Cryptic
Crossword
Puzzles

Cryptic Crossword Puzzles

by Denise Sutherland

A Wiley Brand

Cryptic Crossword Puzzles For Dummies®

Published by

John Wiley & Sons Australia, Ltd
42 McDougall Street
Milton, Qld 4064
www.dummies.com

Copyright © 2020 John Wiley & Sons Australia, Ltd
The moral rights of the author have been asserted.
ISBN 978-0-730-38475-5

A catalogue record for this
book is available from the
National Library of Australia

Cover image: ©Julia Sudnitskaya/Shutterstock

Typeset by SPi

Printed and bound by CPI Group (UK) Ltd, Croydon, CR0 4YY

C9780730384755_260325

The manufacturer's authorized representative according to the EU General Product Safety Regulation is Wiley-VCH GmbH, Boschstr. 12, 69469 Weinheim, Germany, e-mail: Product_Safety@wiley.com.

Contents at a Glance

Introduction

People love to do puzzles of all kinds; word squares, anagrams, number puzzles, riddles, conundrums, jigsaws and so on have entertained and educated people everywhere for thousands of years. And, since 1913, crosswords have held sway.

To anyone new to cryptic crosswords, delight may be rare! On first reading, cryptic crossword clues look like complete and utter gibberish (you call *that* a clue?!). However, cryptic crosswords conform to a set of rules and they *can* be solved. Honest!

About This Book

In this book I give you a brief introduction to cryptic crosswords and provide you with some tips on getting started with these puzzles, the basics of the most common cryptic clue devices, and some useful reference lists. However, the main content of this book is the collection of cryptic crosswords, 56 of them in total.

Foolish Assumptions

I haven't made many assumptions in this book; the main one is that you have some interest in learning to solve cryptic crosswords! I do assume that you have a basic knowledge of grammar (understanding the difference between nouns and verbs, for example, and what plurals, synonyms and adjectives are). But that's about it.

How This Book Is Organised

Cryptic Crossword Puzzles For Dummies is divided into three parts, as follows.

Part 1: The World of Cryptic Crosswords

This part consists of two chapters. The first chapter gives a basic introduction to cryptic crosswords in general, explains the terms and conventions used in crosswords, defines what makes up a cryptic clue, and gives a brief description of each of the main cryptic devices.

The next chapter provides you with some handy reference lists that are very useful when solving cryptic crosswords.

Part 2: Cryptic Crosswords

This part of the book has three chapters of cryptic crosswords for you to sink your teeth into! Chapter 3 has 25 easy cryptic crosswords, Chapter 4 has 18 medium cryptic crosswords, and Chapter 5 has 13 difficult cryptic crosswords.

If you're keen to try more and learn more about solving cryptics, check out the companion volume to this book, *Solving Cryptic Crosswords For Dummies*, which contains in-depth information on solving cryptic crosswords, including how the different cryptic devices work, and more practice puzzles (with hints).

Part 3: The Answers

The part title gives it away, really! This part is a collection of the answers to the cryptics in Chapters 3, 4 and 5.

This book is written in Australian/British English. However, now and then you will see an American spelling in a clue, which was necessary for some wordplay or other to work.

Icons Used in This Book

As is standard with all *For Dummies* books, I use a set of icons to signpost a few special cases within the explanatory chapter. When you come across one of these icons, pay attention to the text next to it:

TIP

This marks a tip or a hint that you might find especially helpful when solving cryptic crosswords.

REMEMBER

This icon helps you to remember a few critical elements about cryptics.

WARNING

These warnings mark out places where getting tripped up is all too easy, as well as common areas of confusion.

Where to Go from Here

This book and the puzzles in it aren't intended to be read or solved from front to back, in order. However, if you're completely new to cryptics, I do recommend you read Chapter 1 first.

From there, each chapter in Part 2 will give you a particular cryptic crossword difficulty level to solve. If you're experienced with cryptics, then dive straight into the hard crosswords in Chapter 5, or work your way up to them, starting with the easy puzzles in Chapter 3.

1

The World of Cryptic Crosswords

In this part, we head straight into the mystifying world of cryptic crosswords! I provide you with some background to this form of brain puzzler, explain what makes a cryptic clue, and reveal the basics of cryptic clue devices and definitions.

After getting through the fundamentals, the next chapter in this part offers handy reference lists of the harder cryptic abbreviations and anagram indicators.

Chapter **1**

Introducing Cryptic Crosswords

n this chapter, I explain to you the absolute basics of cryptic crosswords. I set out the common crossword terminology so you can find your way around the grid with ease, and reveal the anatomy of a cryptic clue. (Stunt clues were used, never fear!) I list the main cryptic clue devices, with brief explanations, and tell you about indicator words.

I've also included a rather handy checklist of my top tips for making a start on any crossword, as well as my top cryptic solving tips.

Getting a Handle on Crossword Terminology

There are a few terms that are good to know when discussing crosswords.

A crossword puzzle consists of a grid of black and white squares, some of which are numbered, and a set of clues placed near the grid.

A letter in the grid that's part of both an across and a down word is said to be *checked*. A letter that's part of just one word is *unchecked*.

Figure 1-1 shows the basic elements of a crossword grid.

In cryptics, the letter count is in brackets at the end of the clue; this tells you how many letters are in the answer. The letter count also tells you whether a hyphen is present in the answer, or the answer contains more than one word, which can be very helpful information.

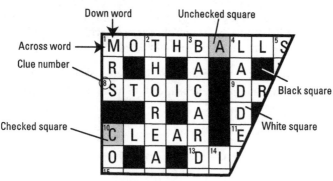

FIGURE 1-1: The basic elements of a crossword grid.

Understanding Clues and Discovering Answers

The initial surface meaning you get when first reading a cryptic clue is intended to mislead you — but not permanently. The tussle between clue writer and clue solver is meant to be a friendly competition, always weighted in your favour. After all, the setter does want you to solve their clues — eventually!

Your task is to see beyond the distracting surface meaning and look for the true meaning of each clue. You need to look at every single word in the clue, one by one, to see what they might mean within the clue, rather than reading the clue as a phrase.

As well as breaking the clue down into its individual words, some other general principles can be applied to most clues to help you. In the following sections, I provide tips on breaking clues down and getting started on working out answers.

Dissecting Cryptic Clues

Each cryptic clue is basically a very concise mini-puzzle. A cryptic clue contains a definition and a bit of wordplay. Yes, you heard right. Cryptic clues contain the definition of the answer, in plain sight, such as you'd find in any quick, non-cryptic, crossword clue. However, cryptic clues also include other elements to point you in the right direction of the answer.

Finding the definition within the clue

The definition may be disguised somewhat, but, trust me, it's there! It resides at the start or end of the clue (not in the middle). A major key to cracking cryptics is to locate the definition within each clue.

The definition part of a cryptic clue may not be an exact dictionary synonym for the answer — it may be off at a slight tangent to it. It does have to be a fair definition, though, and has to match the part of speech of the answer (so a plural answer has to have a plural definition, for example).

The definition part of the clue may be a straight synonym for the answer, or it may require a bit more of a stretch of the imagination, such as *they would be good for picnics* = SAND-WICHES, which clearly isn't a dictionary definition for sandwiches.

Sometimes a definition in a clue presents you with an example of something, and you need to extrapolate the definition from this example. These clues often have *perhaps*, or similar in the clue wording.

So be prepared to look a little further afield for meanings or synonyms for the definition in the clue, because the answer may not be the most obvious word that comes to mind.

The definition part of the clue may also suggest, say, a noun on the surface reading, but in fact be defining a verb.

Having fun with wordplay

The wordplay part of the clue is (hopefully!) where the enjoyment comes in.

Solving the wordplay side of the clue should give you the same answer provided by the definition part of the clue. This means you get confirmation right away that you've got the right answer — something I love about cryptic clues. The wordplay and the definition should both lead to the same answer, and then you get that oh so satisfying 'Ah haaa!' moment.

TIP

Because each cryptic clue contains the definition and a bit of wordplay, once you've figured out which part of the clue is the wordplay element, the remainder of the clue can automatically be pinned down as the definition.

Roughly eight main types of wordplay devices are used in cryptic clues:

>> Anagrams

>> Charades, or linked words

>> Containers, or words inside other words

>> Homophones, or words that sound like other words

>> Reversals

>> Deletions

>> Double definitions

>> Hidden words

At the end of this chapter I give you a very brief run-down on what each clue device is. For a proper discussion about these devices, please see my other book *Solving Cryptic Crosswords For Dummies*.

Looking out for indicator words

Along with the definition and some wordplay, many cryptic clues also include indicator words. These vital words indicate the sort of wordplay device involved.

For example, anagram indicators are words included in the clue like *cooked*, *damaged*, *insane* and *mixed up* — words that indicate you need to alter the letter order of some of the words in the clue to get the answer.

WARNING

While indicator words often highlight the existence of a word-play device in a clue, they may also be a perfectly 'innocent' part of a totally different type of clue, such as the definition. Remember to think of all possibilities when working on clues!

Getting a handle on linking words and punctuation

Even the small words and punctuation used in cryptic clues can be important — or an attempt to slow you down!

Cryptic clues may have linking words in them, which help the clue to read well, and connect the definition and the wordplay to each other. These are generally short words and phrases such as *a*, *and*, *can be*, *from*, *gets*, *has*, *in*, *is*, *reveals*, *with* and *yielding* (among many others). Not all clues have them, however, so depending on whose crosswords you're solving, you may come across these a lot, or not often at all.

Linking words usually give a sense of equality (this equals that), or show that one part of the clue results in the other. Keep in mind, though, that a word that looks like a linking word might be another part of the clue, such as part of the definition, or anagram fodder.

Another thing to be aware of is punctuation in clues — it's generally there to confuse you, and make the superficial meaning read better. In general, it's safe to ignore it. A question mark can sometimes indicate a need to think a bit more laterally. An apostrophe s ('s) is often an abbreviation of *is*.

Appreciating abbreviations

Abbreviations are widely used in cryptic clues, to add one or a few letters to the wordplay. Thousands of words can be used as 'abbreviation indicators'. Most of these are abbreviations you are familiar with, such as *right* = R and *east* = E. However, many are more unusual. For example, *first* = IST, because it looks a bit like 1st. There is a list of some abbreviations in Chapter 2. Getting the common abbreviations under your belt will really help you crack the cryptic code!

Putting it All Together

Launching into a real cryptic clue can help you get a feel for the different elements within the clue. Take, for example, the following:

Knave's wild dog is missing Al (4)

On first reading, I'm trying to make you imagine a villain's wild dog pining for his mate, Al. This is the surface meaning — try to ignore this imagery!

In this case, the definition is *Knave*, and the wordplay is *wild dog is missing Al*. The clue should be read as, 'A *wild dog* without *Al* also means *knave*.' Can you see the answer? Yes, it's JACK (JACKAL without AL).

Planning Your Attack

Here are my tips for making a start on any crossword:

>> Don't try to do the clues in order. Any answer you can put into the grid makes it easier for you to solve the words that cross over.

>> Draw a hyphen or bar on the grid when a clue's letter count shows the answer is hyphenated or more than one word.

>> Check out the letter count, looking for shorter or very long words. Shorter words can be the easier words to guess, but so too can long words as they have fewer possible solutions.

>> Look for clues where the answer looks like it may be a plural and pencil in an S at the end of these clues.

>> If an answer you're pencilling in to the grid results in an unlikely letter pattern in the crossing-over word, sorry to say, but your answer may be wrong.

>> If you're very stuck on a clue, leave it for a while. Often the answer suddenly seems completely obvious, after a break!

TIP

Here's a list of tips specifically for solving cryptic crosswords:

>> The definition of the answer is in the clue, either at the start or end of the clue.

>> If you think you know what the answer may be (just from the definition), see if you can work backwards from it to figure out whether the wordplay section of the clue fits your answer.

>> Look at each word in the clue one by one, rather than together as a sentence. Don't ignore a single word! Many words indicate abbreviations, and lead to one or two letters (such as *north* = N).

>> It's generally safe to ignore most punctuation and all capital letters in clues.

>> The definition has to match the part of speech and tense of the answer.

>> Use a thesaurus to look for synonyms for words near the start or end of a clue.

>> Practise and practise and practise. This is a difficult puzzle genre, it takes time to improve.

Touching on Cryptic Devices

There isn't room here to go into the workings of each cryptic device in detail (see *Solving Cryptic Crosswords For Dummies* for in-depth explanations and practice crosswords). However, I have put together this little list to help you remember the basics of each clue type, and what sort of words are used as indicators for each device.

Anagrams

The letters to be jumbled up (the fodder) are in plain view in the clue. Abbreviations can be included in the fodder. Indicators give a sense of being awkward, broken, confused, jumbled, mad, mixed, rebuilt, sick and so on. The longest words in a grid often have anagram clues.

Charades

One part comes after another in order, adding up to give the answer and abbreviations are often used.

Indicator words are not generally found in these clues; when used, they give a sense of things being added on, or coming one after the other. This is a very common clue device, and it is often used in conjunction with other devices.

Containers

This is another very common cryptic device, and can be used in combination with other devices. One word, or set of letters, is put inside another word or set of letters. Indicator words give a sense of insertion or containment, or of being put inside or within something else.

Homophones

Homophones are a less common cryptic device, and a crossword may have none, or just one or two.

The answer sounds the same as a different word, but they are spelt differently and mean different things. Indicators include words that give a sense of things being spoken, broadcast, noisy, or listened to.

Reversals

A whole word, or a set of letters, is reversed to form another word, or part of a word in these clue types. Indicators of reversals are words that give a sense of things being reversed, backwards, sent back, and so on. This is a common cryptic device, and often used in conjunction with other devices.

Deletions

With this device, letters are deleted from words to get to the answer. Indicators are words that give a sense of something being cut off, lost, removed, and so on. Letter position can also be indicated with words such as head, finally, middle, borders, half, and so on.

This is a very common device, and is often used in conjunction with other cryptic devices.

Substitutions are a rarer form of deletions, where one letter is substituted for another. Indicator words such as for, instead of, replacing, and so on are used.

Double definitions

These clue devices present two definitions for the same word, one after the other. No other wordplay is used, and they can be very short.

Double definition clues don't usually have indicator words, apart from a few words like and, but, for, gives, makes, or, and that.

Hidden words

This is a less common clue device. Hidden word clues have the answers within the clue, in plain view. The answer is hidden amongst the letters of words in the clue. Sometimes the words are hidden as alternating letters. Indicator words give a sense of containment.

Abbreviations

Abbreviations are widely used in all cryptic crosswords. Many words in cryptic clues lead to abbreviations of one or a few letters. Looking up single letter entries in a dictionary will reveal many of them. Learning the commonly used cryptic abbreviations will help your skill in solving cryptics enormously.

Chapter **2**

Reference Lists

I n this chapter I provide you with some basic reference lists that will help you to crack the clues in this book. Because of space considerations (I wanted to give you as many crosswords as possible!), the lists are very abridged, and just focus on the harder abbreviations and anagram indicators. For more in-depth reference lists, check out *Solving Cryptic Crosswords For Dummies* and my website www.sutherland-studios.com.au.

Abbreviations

Straightforward abbreviations (such as the periodic table, phonetic alphabet, American states, *street* = ST, *east* = E, *right* = R, and *litre* = L) and simple foreign words have been omitted from this list. If you look at the single letter entries in any dictionary, they will provide you with more information.

Simple phrase books, dictionaries and online word lists will help you translate any foreign words in the clues in the book.

10 = X	*Capone* = AL
100 = C	*carbon copy* = CC
1,000 = M	*castle* = R (rook)
5 = V	*chapter* = C or CH
50 = L	*chief* = CH
a follower = B	*Church of England* = CE
about = C, CE, RE	*civil engineer* = CE
against = V (versus)	*cross* = X
alien = ET	*club/s* = C (cards)
American soldier = GI	*Common Era* = CE
ancient city = UR	*Cyprus* = CY
ancient times = BC	*daughter* = D
Anglo-Saxon = AS	*degree* = D, BA, MA
Arabic = AR	*diamond/s* = D (cards)
artist = RA (Royal Academy)	*Diana* = DI
Asian = E (Eastern)	*direction* = N, S, E,W
at home = IN	*doctor* = DR, MB, MD, MO
bishop = B (chess)	*dram* = DR
Bond's boss = M	*duck* = O (cricketing)
book = B	*Elizabeth* = E
bridge player = N, S, E, W	*English* = E
British = B, BR	*exercise* = PT or PE

exist = BE

fine = F (pencil), OK

first = IST (1st)

first class = AI (A1)

fish = LING, EEL, COD etc

force = F

former partner = EX

France = F

gas = H (hydrogen),
CO (carbon monoxide), etc.

George = G

Georgia = GA (state),
GE (country)

German = G

gold = AU or OR (heraldry)

good = G

good man = ST (saint)

graduate = BA, MB

Greek character or letter = PI,
NU, MU, XI, etc.

Guevara = CHE

hard = H (pencil)

heart/s = H (cards)

hexadecimal = HEX

honour = OBE

hour = HR

hug = O

husband = H

hush = SH

I am = IM (I'm)

in charge = IC

instant message = IM

integrated circuit = IC

judge = J

king = K or ER

kiss = X

last character = Z

lawyer = BL (Bachelor of Law)

letter = EF, EM, EL

Liberal = L

line = L (l looks like a line)

loud = F (forte)

midday = N (noon)

model = T (Model T Ford)

moment = MO

monsieur = M

months = MOS

new = N

newton = N (unit)

no good = NG

noon = N

note = A – G, DO, RE, MI, FA, SO, LA, TI, TE, DOH, etc.

nothing = O

ocean = O

old = O

old boy = OB

old city = UR

old record = EP

one = A, AN, I (1)

operation = OP

oriental = E (from the East)

penny = P

playing = ON (stage)

point = N, S, E or W

power = P

present day = AD

princess = DI

printer's measure = EN, EM

private investigator = PI

physical education = PE

Public Record Office = PRO

quarter = N, NE, NW, E etc

queen = R, Q, or ER

queen's honour = OBE

quiet = P (piano)

ring = O

resistance = R (unit)

river = R, EXE, DEE, PO, etc.

roughly = CA (circa)

round = O

sailor, salt = AB (able-bodied seaman)

second = S

second-class = B

Shakespearean king = LEAR

ship/s = SS

short time = T

single = I (1)

society = S

soft = P (music), B (pencil)

son = S

spade/s = S (cards)

square = S

teetotal/ler = TT

temperature = T

thanks = TA

the thing = IT

times = X

top class = AI (A1)

translator = TR

unknown = X or Y

versus = V, VS

very black = BB (pencil)

vitamin = A, B, BI (B1), C, etc.

vote = X

wife = W

will = LL (contraction)

women's supporter = BRA

worker = ANT, BEE

year = Y

yours truly = I, ME

Anagram Indicators

This list contains a few of the less obvious anagram indicators. Any word that gives a sense of letters being moved around, rearranged, abused, organised, broken, constructed, unusual, active, ugly, sick, upset, confused, changed, cooked, weird, insane, messy, surprising, or even drunk, can generally be an anagram indicator.

abandoned	artfully	batty
about	astonishing	boiled
abysmal	at sea	building
acrobatic	awkward	bungled
after a fashion	bad	burst
amazing	bananas	busy
amendment	bashed	cocktail
anomalous	battered	complex

composition	floundering	performs
construction	flying	perverse
corrupt	forged	pie
criminal	hammered	plastic
crooked	hideously	preparation
cruelly	high	ruin
curiously	hit	rum
designed	ill-bred	scrappy
desperate	intricate	scratched
developed	kind of	shape
disguised	ludicrous	somehow
distilled	mash	soup
elaborate	maybe	special
elastic	mysterious	stray
engineer	nasty	tidy up
exotic	naughty	treatment
fabricated	new	turning
fancy	nimble	twisted
fantastic	novel	unhappily
fishy	obstreperous	version
flexible	ornate	wicked

2

Cryptic
Crosswords

Chapter **3**
Easy Peasy Cryptics

've done my best to write easy crosswords for you in this chapter. These crosswords have easy words in the grids and simpler vocabulary in the clues as well. Abbreviations are (hopefully) mostly pretty obvious. The clues use more anagrams and hidden word devices than normal, which are in general easier clues to solve. Many words in the clues are presented 'in plain view', and you don't have to find synonyms for them. The grids are also smaller than a regular crossword (13 × 13, instead of 15 × 15). I hope you enjoy them!

Puzzle 1

Across

1. Put Rover in lead to get to an adage (7)
5. Cyprus cad's ancient plant (5)
8. Carries large mammals (5)
9. Illustration shows Diana with silver ram (7)
10. Glib excuse covers wild goat (4)
11. Lack of courage? Muddled Dimity has it (8)
13. Strange hen meowed, only to get vine fruit (8,5)
16. Disloyalty from dodgy early bat (8)
17. Badly cure fawn (4)
20. Exercise caution in public sale (7)
21. American state set in lah-di-dah oasis (5)
22. Sidestep a stray dog in Delaware (5)
23. Drive backwards to wild reserve (7)

Down

1. Bishop and Long Island in push to bring out a book (7)
2. Astatine found in mineral source? Make a speech! (5)
3. Warped seat where the sun rises (4)
4. Bad bends remained, revealing doctor's attitude to patient (7,6)
5. Sloppy archaism has charm (8)
6. Pleasant drink concentrate (7)
7. Stout jumpy daughter for Juliet (5)
12. Erratic damn yeti has explosive (8)
14. Saw it's not frosted (7)
15. Upset, rue neon nerve cell (7)
16. Soft ground is tasteless (5)
18. Seat 100 next to locks (5)
19. Ukrainian city infiltrated by Coxsackie virus (4)

Puzzle 2

Across

1. Looking around, trying to find missing centre (6)
4. Ceremonial female, or Malcolm? (6)
7. Warped latitude produces elevation (8)
8. The French doctor identifies the baby sheep (4)
9. Lied badly and became lazy (4)
11. Vaguely ban new style (8)
13. Malingering one has terribly achy chin droop (13)
18. Pa reflected on dainty hunger (8)
21. Downhearted among singing lumberjacks (4)
23. Part of the eye's flower (4)
24. Ocean identified in student article, found in attic (8)
25. Abnormal uterus gets surgical stitch (6)
26. Amble along to southern cave-dwelling creature (6)

Down

1. Smash his pans from Madrid (7)
2. Rave about core of next Olympians (5)
3. Go to university and beat the Hungarian stew (7)
4. Worries about guitar features (5)
5. Mattered to me and worker (5)
6. Hit ball by entrance hall (5)
10. Scapegoat hid sense of self (3)
12. Decapitated bloodsucker's grassy area (3)
14. Give money back for bark (3)
15. The French filling needs for sewing implements (7)
16. Mat cuts top off medicine (3)
17. Funny Mike is in ragged calico (7)
18. Remarkably arise to see constellation (5)
19. Hideously inapt whitewash (5)
20. Picture one mage (5)
22. Bingo held in the lot, tomorrow (5)

Puzzle 3

Across

1. Maria plus weird kangaroo, perhaps? (9)

8. Weep for graduate with western student (4)

9. Retain possession of fortress tower (4)

10. Shattered prism lost soft edges (4)

12. Beaten without first being consumed (5)

14. Roast Alaska in bed (5)

16. An odd apple for primate (3)

17. Sited and set audit poorly (8)

20. Bag the Spanish roll (5)

21. Memento of our vines smashed (8)

22. Set on fire, and left it (3)

23. Track down broken crate (5)

25. Place an ad in Brazilian city for a transceiver (5)

28. Looked back to quiet insect (4)

30. Oddly unsteady and pre-owned (4)

31. The Italian Zulu unknown is lethargic (4)

32. For now, e-mail when busy (9)

Down

2. Wise men miss leader for long times (4)

3. Brown Greek letter dropped into the sea (5)

4. Freely smear pan with hard cheese (8)

5. Work the land, without first limb (3)

6. Rapidly go without food (4)

7. Surprisingly bland diet for mysterious rendezvous (5,4)

11. Korean capital's soul has energy (5)

13. Slowly cook diced escaroles (9)

14. Boyfriend talks about decorative ribbon (4)

15. Cultivate it with a finger (5)

18. Strangely pert Rain Turtle (8)

19. Story end read aloud (4)

20. Under ugly elbow (5)

24. 100 hurry to make a crowd (5)

26. Labyrinth with daughter rather than Mike can stupefy (4)

27. Stagger and leer in lift (4)

29. Contest lost first high card (3)

Puzzle 4

Across

1. Lob moss carelessly and come into flower (7)
5. Tries out cricket matches (5)
8. Damp turnover in ship fricassees (5)
9. Pastoral wall painting, with a castle for 1,000 (5)
10. Buffoon regularly identifies a flying saucer (3)
11. Upset cousin hugs hotel pillow (7)
13. Ancient city ban is the opposite of 9 across (5)
14. Cracked cog teeth cease to make dairy product (7,6)
17. Sprinted to church property (5)
19. Self-satisfied, note the French sneak in goods (7)
23. Insect's pants missing edges (3)
24. Connection to the web — 'Fashion with Mike' (5)
25. Bud to rehash indecision (5)
26. Surprisingly, cadre's concerned (5)
27. Mad Hot Dory is Toto's owner (7)

Down

1. Spartan computing language (5)
2. Accepts orders from old boy with an unexpected yes (5)
3. Japanese snack? Squish madly without question! (5)
4. Misapprehend Martin's sudden confusion (13)
5. Audibly flung to the other side (7)
6. Scour the undergrowth (5)
7. The Italian in a chaotic scene is quiet (7)
12. Beret, for example, can be found in Manhattan (3)
14. Novel car mice are made of clay (7)
15. Embarrassed Ed has Ma out of sorts (7)
16. Veggie extract is an omelette ingredient (3)
18. Lowest level drain broken (5)
20. One from Paris and the German are below (5)
21. Some of the gaga untouchables are emaciated (5)
22. The gentry leave their leader behind, and get admission (5)

Puzzle 5

Across

1. Resident involved in solo callisthenics (5)
4. Flip over the boat hat dimensions (7)
8. Drop from an aircraft? Badly hurt apace! (9)
9. Nap for a Lao dollar (3)
10. Lamer hectic kingdom (5)
11. Sees grasping alien husband, and is furious (7)
13. Administer drugs, unhurried (6)
15. Stables are tall in ships (6)
17. Dancing Peter with Foxtrot Charlie is ideal (7)
18. Dismisses back-to-front letter feature (5)
20. Even one annoys, oddly (3)
22. Plant matter comes from blended louse cell (9)
23. Nastily destroys headless bivalves (7)
24. Modelled and refined Ed's op (5)

Down

1. Repel rising social outcast (5)
2. Adorn rice anew with spice (9)
3. Stand-in doctor tipped over the Mucol (5)
4. Elaborate cure is to take a sea trip (6)
5. Give a gift (7)
6. Irritate with nitrogen, instead of right pen's medium (3)
7. Reveals corrupt ex-posse (7)
12. Our hail is haphazard and so funny! (9)
13. Horribly soon, rap with singer (7)
14. Broken eel cart produces dark syrup (7)
16. Loony lusty Sierra gets a pen-like device (6)
18. First umpire hides part of the wicket (5)
19. Companion lost Romeo to a villain (5)
21. Absolutely unknown Asian soprano (3)

Puzzle 6

Across

1. Emotional release from abnormal cat's hairs (9)
6. Fish found inside a crocodile (3)
8. Bright bulb lit up unsteadily (5)
9. Small part of a plant's brochure (7)
10. Husband with the old sodium supplies laughing scavenger (5)
11. Disorganised fair can come from Algeria, perhaps? (7)
13. I've heard Parisian river is lucid (4)
15. Peculiar ten gum spice (6)
16. Pill battle blown up (6)
19. Arrival misses the middle inland sea (4)
21. Dubious respect for a ghost (7)
24. Caught noisy atmospheric mass (5)
25. Carports have petrol covering broken gears (7)
26. Shaggy fairy gets husband for female (5)
28. Digit caught in photoelectrics (3)
29. Flexible tile resin all over the place (9)

Down

1. Feline half of cattle (3)
2. Highest mobile satellite lost energy unit (7)
3. Placate with a very quiet calmness (7)
4. Muslim ruler's dried grape finally gone (6)
5. 'Look at that,' he said — 'A step!' (5)
6. Little brother left cooked broccoli, it causes abdominal pain (5)
7. Ted atoned insanely, and exploded! (9)
10. Understanding from experience with stewed night dish (9)
12. Greek cheese wrapped in taffeta (4)
14. Gallium put into argon makes marine gel (4)
17. Weird local hotel has zero booze (7)
18. Noel goes up to island north east, like a big cat (7)
20. Operates again rescues at sea without Charlie (6)
22. Sinister eastern Great Lake (5)
23. Striped cat's good in a row (5)
27. Nevertheless, the Abominable Snowman is tailless (3)

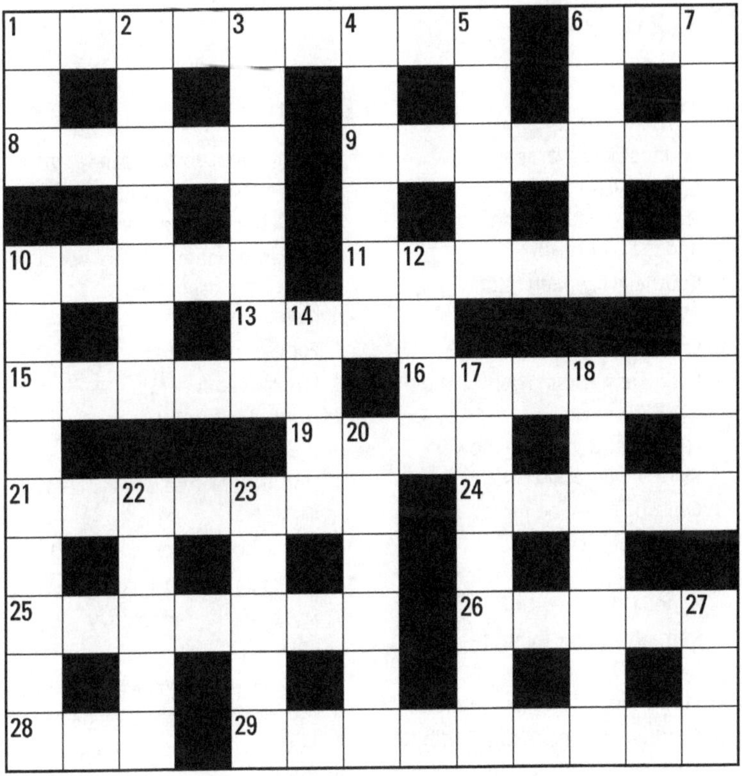

Puzzle 7

Across

1. Sounds like royal seat launched! (6)
4. Remove husband from car body and get a drink (6)
9. Southern Egyptian region essential to Ainu biathlon (5)
10. Cost of flying to fancy Era Fair (7)
11. Little Aussie state recalled the S.A.T. (3)
12. Hotel is after a showy flower from the Emerald Isle (5)
13. Obliging husband fell up accidentally (7)
15. Fever gauge's theorem term edited (11)
21. Remade caliper for scale model (7)
24. Play under par, bird of prey! (5)
25. Graduate George's carryall (3)
26. Mistakenly rile hag who supplies coiffure product (4,3)
27. Stop sleeping and have a weak cocktail (5)
28. I tarry badly to get collector's item (6)
29. Hasten, intoxicated, to Greek capital (6)

Down

1. Astringent substance in tea's brown at home back north (6)
2. Rush bib out to garbage (7)
3. He jumps into turbulent water to get the atmospheric conditions (7)
5. Foolish month (5)
6. Employees stick (5)
7. Dodgy lass holds a note for thieves (6)
8. Unorthodox Abalone Fish is in *Vogue* (11)
14. Stroke companion animal (3)
16. Long fish is even in cereals! (3)
17. Stylish alien grabs messy angel (7)
18. Inscribe nasty avenger (7)
19. Legendary British king's hart lost near ancient city (6)
20. Seamstresses make drains (6)
22. Franciscan head has previous! (5)
23. Precious bar pocketed in a redingote (5)

Puzzle 8

Across

1. Wear a costume provided by wicked red puss (5,2)
5. Year round leave maypole tree (5)
8. Set aside cannula that's missing edges (5)
9. Feels remorse for right herons (7)
10. Flat and unfit, lacking force (4)
11. Thickens stews in cooking areas (8)
13. Something like a strange expiatory lamp (13)
16. Irregular rain came from Texas, perhaps? (8)
17. Gelato fudge contains a soy product (4)
20. Badly stab Ma with Indian rice (7)
21. Sang about learner's informal speech (5)
22. Unstable truss corrodes (5)
23. Cooked retsina is more awful (7)

Down

1. Vampire's dual car in pieces (7)
2. Tedium from eleven nuisances (5)
3. Transaction to go by sea, I've heard (4)
4. Involvement in organised patriotic pain (13)
5. Weird maniac hugs American soldier conjuror (8)
6. Lead up to unconventional creed involved in physical education (7)
7. Turbulent sea in El Salvador subsides (5)
12. Vacations with wriggly oily shad (8)
14. Makes happy with parking rentals (7)
15. Oscar on broken gurney is less mature (7)
16. Honey-yellow bream mixture (5)
18. Okay ace private investigator represents giraffe's relative (5)
19. Egyptian goddess heads off catastrophe (4)

Puzzle 9

Across

1. Misshape bananas from Ed (6)
4. Bubble gets an A for university chatter (6)
7. Progeny lend rich cocktail (8)
8. Pa concealing student with oriental entreaty (4)
9. Turning soil yields grain store (4)
11. Start off with mad dietitian, who lost her head (8)
13. Cool down bent rare fig tree (11)
16. Go towards a very quiet roach (8)
19. Mist coming from Hotel Arizona East (4)
22. Dock heath (4)
23. Sleeping pill mixture deviates (8)
24. Sweet seen in packet of feed (6)
25. Distinguished month (6)

Down

1. Evades waterbirds (5)
2. Top up around queen's ruffle (5)
3. Cocktail for drunk mini rat (7)
4. Sydney beach covered by carbon dioxide (5)
5. Bravo! A trainee gets South Australia's timber (5)
6. Rub out right in facility (5)
10. Rough bloke lost start of loaf (3)
12. Peg's odd theme (3)
13. Hit artist quietly (3)
14. Spiny Aussie had nice soup (7)
15. Tree's embers (3)
16. Da and Tim both climbing up to be let in (5)
17. Evidence of a piano on the top of the house? (5)
18. Talk about a little island's passage (5)
20. A princess gets English university's farewell (5)
21. Vent after Asian function (5)

Puzzle 10

Across

1. Plated animal's messy modallair (9)

8. Slack hobble (4)

9. Champion's sample of mother-of-pearl (4)

10. Work on textiles half gone (4)

12. Grown weirdly in error (5)

14. Harm surrounds eastern women's quarters (5)

16. Consumed eight, from the sound of it (3)

17. Tolerance shown by those waiting for the doctor on the phone (8)

20. Jo gets involved in clamour for French mustard (5)

21. Desperately urged Don, but he's unlikely to win (8)

22. Assess the animal doctor (3)

23. Depend on locking up pawn to get an answer (5)

25. Dark blood group shortage (5)

28. Inscribe 'tech' awkwardly (4)

30. Taxonomy covers part of nerve cell (4)

31. Sicilian volcano is strangely neat (4)

32. Insanely chain tsar to insurgent (9)

Down

2. Deer runs back to get plant (4)

3. Pleasant fragrance is a feature of taro macaroons (5)

4. Adventurous diner? Tip at random! (8)

5. The French kiss is slipshod (3)

6. American spies get round to an Italian greeting (4)

7. Mash Pat's eight strands of pasta (9)

11. American author from Washington gets into tin (5)

13. Treasures suave ball dancing (9)

14. Her daughter got a group of cattle (4)

15. Senior officer to wander back, embracing Juliet (5)

18. Eccentric ghetto queen is level-headed (8)

19. Blue Avenue in New York (4)

20. Sir Francis' duck (5)

24. Reluctant to discover a Liberal promise (5)

26. Haggard, missing first relation (4)

27. Notice reversed shirts (4)

29. Gold-brown one found in Tennessee (3)

Puzzle 11

Across

1. Unusually good plasma light that's old fashioned (3,4)

5. Dancing bi lad can speak off the cuff (2,3)

8. Leaderless people get drunk and marry in secret (5)

9. Perplex with a labyrinth (5)

10. Vehicle is a feature of healthcare (3)

11. Beast chewed up mentors (7)

13. Best possible agreement after one (5)

14. Recollections about misguided incense crimes (13)

17. Moved nearer to old carved jewellery piece (5)

19. Examine insect eating phosphorous (7)

23. Uproar from dinosaur! (3)

24. No difficulty to line artist's frame (5)

25. Small flying mammal he can wash (5)

26. Posts small stubs (5)

27. Mere lad remodelled the green gem (7)

Down

1. Learner in the confusing game gets a glimmer (5)

2. Faint quickly around whiskey (5)

3. A Delaware exercise expert (5)

4. Disguised rioter catnaps to play for time (13)

5. Extreme greed for mixed caviare (7)

6. Rental agreement for renovated 24A (5)

7. Les after root vegetable insects (7)

12. Cut short uncontrolled slide to go over snow (3)

14. Restock demolished missiles (7)

15. Back soon, hugging daughter, who has the French pasta (7)

16. Even unhappy to doze . . . (3)

18. Stone worker's mother has a male child (5)

20. Bears crooked sword (5)

21. Additional English vote on art retrospective (5)

22. We divide Ted's cloth (5)

Puzzle 12

Across

1. Stallion's sounding rough, I hear (5)

4. Seychelles Member of Parliament Tom gets an indication (7)

8. Rebuke bad imp — ran red! (9)

9. Mythical bird's stone tail chipped off (3)

10. Gulliver's creator is fast (5)

11. Exotic Elm is so supple (7)

13. Irritable, like a crustacean? (6)

15. Messed up maturely — forgot Gold Eucalyptus, perhaps? (6)

17. Italian herb and old orange mixed up (7)

18. Platform yard has a white flower (5)

20. Corner missing new berth (3)

22. Alert, yet tentative at sea (9)

23. Fowl and duck included in work schedule (7)

24. Inflexible, I can be put in crude grid (5)

Down

1. Sherbets don't include set of aromatic plants (5)

2. Reproduce from mutated elite carp (9)

3. Decree cited revision (5)

4. Main paper fastener (6)

5. Method with pigpen produces humility (7)

6. Large rodent runs up sticky liquid (3)

7. Teach me acrobatics with a broad knife (7)

12. Getting big nation amendment (9)

13. Jemmy's black bird next to a tavern (7)

14. Flagrant bishop left at worker (7)

16. New Forest is more marshy (6)

18. Diana ran back to get Iranian currency (5)

19. Produce from unusual Yankee deli (5)

21. A bit of an assiduous pair! (3)

Puzzle 13

Across

1. Building gap as goal for Pacific archipelago (9)

6. Large snake regularly seen in baobab (3)

8. Very liberal translator seen in the Ukraine (5)

9. I left neutrino disrupted, to find another subatomic particle (7)

10. Ink all over iron blade (5)

11. Keenly, Georgia got in ahead of time (7)

13. Prohibits from pubs (4)

15. UK city's 50 playing Bradman (6)

16. Wild typhoon shed unknown light particle (6)

19. Heads off nauseous plain sailing (4)

21. Drunken brawl on with bird of prey (4,3)

24. Sweetheart is after golf hand protection (5)

25. Deport old battered missile (7)

26. Sample of spaniel bow-wow's joint (5)

28. Yes, Spanish Romeo's formal address (3)

29. Segregate corrupt bunny's gift (6,3)

Down

1. Wildebeest understood, by the sounds of it (3)

2. Jaunty, valiant one from Riga (7)

3. Pulverised pale cob for an experimental control (7)

4. George and the Queen get a male goose (6)

5. Daze German, injured by an insect (5)

6. Tedious insect that makes holes? (5)

7. Ludicrous! Anyone can be a nuisance! (9)

10. Tykes boil reconditioned memory units (9)

12. Gasps 'Headless vipers!' (4)

14. A north-eastern wife, once again (4)

17. Tidy up nigh, with eye to personal cleanliness (7)

18. Problems? Ring in versatile butler! (7)

20. Gives permission to Capone, with batty owls (6)

22. More bloody steak is scarcer (5)

23. Corpulent queen's honour goes to soprano and Asian (5)

27. Swigger wears a toupee (3)

Puzzle 14

Across

1. Chapter in total edited for *Little Women* author (6)

4. Outlandish ideal Eastern Penguin (6)

9. All went back after six to the country house (5)

10. Recover from an amazing miracle (7)

11. Regularly wrote of great sorrow (3)

12. California sheltering Middle East's desert animal (5)

13. Do without salt blemish (7)

15. Rewritten soccer intro leads to improvements (11)

21. Rum bees mistreated the Asian cat (7)

24. World's molten heart (5)

25. Flow back among pebbles (3)

26. Cavorting chis run to ragamuffins (7)

27. Avoid advertisement collected by Eve (5)

28. UK county ruin sorted (6)

29. A German husband? A saint is horrified! (6)

Down

1. Modern day immorality leads to counselling (6)

2. Sri Lankan capital's combo travelled around lake circuit (7)

3. Fish boat from Turkey gets Awl Queen (7)

5. Removes ports (5)

6. Shopping centre raised one pack animal (5)

7. White stoat comes from the King Quarry (6)

8. Dynamic ace scheme re dairy food! (5,6)

14. Pair depicted in artwork (3)

16. Caught up in ephemeral sleep state (1,1,1)

17. One cold grebe reversed Titanic's nemesis (7)

18. Cobain's band in paradise (7)

19. Ridiculous zany rad bus (6)

20. About intercepting that warning . . . (6)

22. Motorsport driver's ace in Rolls Royce (5)

23. The Spanish tangled neckwear is best (5)

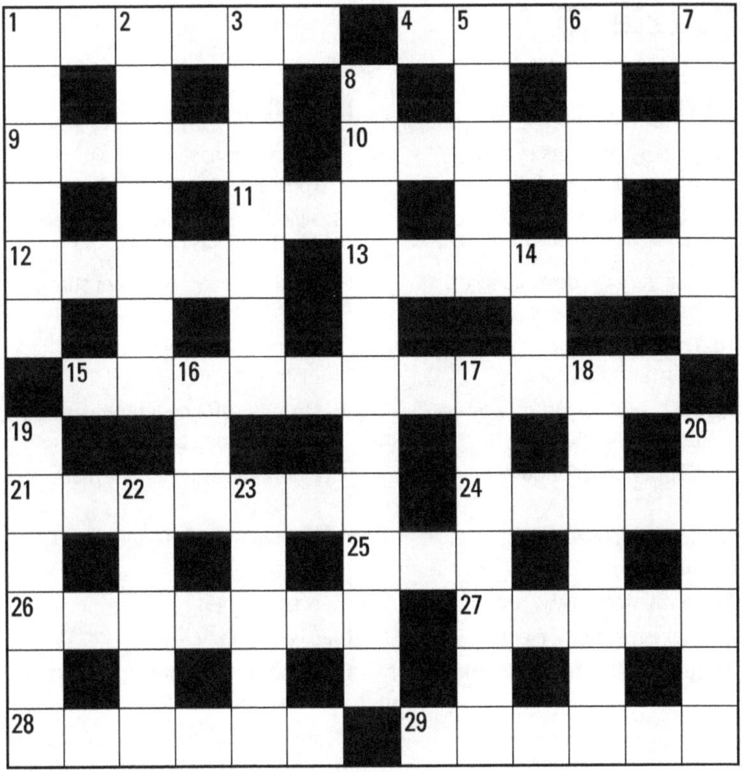

Puzzle 15

Across

1. Wild python gets to first mesmerist (9)

8. Missed start of march to curved structure (4)

9. Contrary cat devours a litre of perfumed powder (4)

10. Following former partner in the Northern Territory (4)

12. Tests axe the wrong way on manuscript (5)

14. Copper alloy found right inside a fish (5)

16. Sounds like actor Grant's colour (3)

17. Demented bag got on sledge (8)

20. Make mention of, either way (5)

21. Red American bird's number (8)

22. Small rug has an impact, even (3)

23. Because it's part of a disincentive (5)

25. Judge leaves the mysterious jungle to pounce! (5)

28. Ripped up accommodation fee (4)

30. Foul smell from stream primarily gone (4)

31. Tango victory for identical sibling (4)

32. Arduous tune sours badly (9)

Down

2. Unknown eastern Arabic twelve-month period (4)

3. Agitated prince loses his head, and becomes friendlier (5)

4. Light filament metal net stung dreadfully (8)

5. Soprano has ace times with instrument (3)

6. Drunken affair, without very loud operatic song (4)

7. Nuts Guevara takes on mad stunts (9)

11. Singer changed toner (5)

13. Confectionary loot cache is organised (9)

14. Live on King Ale (4)

15. Couches one note after another with soprano (5)

18. Denigrate till beet disintegrates (8)

19. Courageous pastime (4)

20. Flower that holds water (5)

24. Bedraggled cur of Greek island (5)

26. Sodium on the Italian pin (4)

27. Guys have uniform bill of fare (4)

29. Baby newt's left leaderless (3)

1
2
3
4
5
6
7
8
9
10
11
12
13
14
15
16
17
18
19
20
21
22
23
24
25
26
27
28
29
30
31
32

Puzzle 16

Across

1. Doctor lets out roadside lodgings (6)

4. Anxious about fair ad arrangement (6)

7. Reduce 501 Minis next to hotel (8)

8. Oscar and wife residing in Tennessee's settlement (4)

9. Stand over with a weaving device (4)

11. Give details of French secretary (8)

13. Roan bug dove, flailing, into some kind of swimming pool (5,6)

16. Messily open oats with kitchen utensil (8)

19. Poland to back secret plan (4)

22. Object in Counterfeit Emporium (4)

23. Pink bird's burning with oxygen (8)

24. Fresh rare south-eastern rubber (6)

25. Sabotage one ark from Seoul (6)

Down

1. Male love of the Italian replica (5)

2. Met in lift at Post Office to get speed (5)

3. Welds in tangled fleece (7)

4. Unexpected chase results in dull pains (5)

5. King Victor left ravioli and garlic mayonnaise (5)

6. I abandoned the author of this book, she's impenetrable! (5)

10. Earth's satellite cut short cow's noise (3)

12. Naughty part of Barbados! (3)

13. Heard about a raw mineral wonder (3)

14. A crank's deplorable plunder (7)

15. Short referee is endlessly jumpy (3)

16. Fashionable, in ornate wet string (5)

17. Assembled near a stadium (5)

18. Provide a strong box missing its top (5)

20. Horseman's spear is clean, surprisingly (5)

21. Short time on antler spike (5)

Puzzle 17

Across

1. Take heart! It's mixed here, in a cup (5,2)
5. Ascot complex serves Mexican snacks (5)
8. Rinse poorly, get alarm bell! (5)
9. Lock bag unexpectedly, it causes a build-up of work (7)
10. Accomplice is sort of loyal, without love (4)
11. Queen's Australian state (8)
13. Heaven's editor cooked a light British meal (10,3)
16. Atrocious bloc leak can be secured! (8)
17. Threesome come from Thailand and Brazilian state (4)
20. Shuddering, eased in to black jellybean flavour (7)
21. Give nickname to first class Arabic emirate (5)
22. Requires dense novel (5)
23. Shouting and lying afresh around the Spanish (7)

Down

1. Stir at curds to make a milky dessert (7)
2. Sign up confused loner (5)
3. Chime from band (4)
4. Upset, duly chop alibi time off for everyone (6,7)
5. Unforthcoming cat ran back to island turn (8)
6. Criminal cult hiding bad rip (7)
7. Greek letter to tenor leaves stigma (5)
12. American runners from Alaska wearing cruel smiles (8)
14. A carbon copy dividing vine immunisation (7)
15. Cherishing marriage token following commotion (7)
16. Discover renal disturbance (5)
18. Jewish scholar's bunny lost its tail (5)
19. Celebrity found among wildfowl, even! (4)

Puzzle 18

Across

3. Noticed the hand tool (3)

7. Maybe come around eleven to see Central American country (6)

8. Automate arrangement without Ma, to dine at a restaurant (3,3)

9. Doctor included in strange decree for a month (8)

10. Flower's oily, left for nothing (4)

11. Part of indomitable Miss (4)

13. Blend of opposites is my fuel, strangely! (8)

15. Wrapping operation found in Version Eleven (8)

16. Whip up iced game cubes (4)

17. Impale the Saint Sailor (4)

18. Revolts at absence of gusts? (8)

20. Poke at bustling capital of Kansas (6)

21. The Italian fool's lake (6)

22. Megastore contains helium, for example (3)

Down

1. Flexibly orientate mind's will power (13)

2. Smooth portfolio (4)

3. Ornate brooms hide concerning hat from 7A (8)

4. Have on, leaving off first promise (4)

5. Awkward sly edits done in a mannered way (8)

6. Certificate in AquaFit Coil exercising (13)

12. Doctor trainee is among trees; shakes like a leaf (8)

14. Weirdly uses lint with gadgets (8)

18. Doctor has silver haul (4)

19. Spur on, even in outrigger (4)

Puzzle 19

Across

2. Strangely loves to find the solution (5)

7. Be servile to the baby deer (4)

8. Speak indistinctly to the mule harbouring a doctor (6)

9. Squished endless tropical stone fruit (7)

10. Drop off peels in return (5)

12. Morning drops among trade wind (3)

13. Account with curate is correct (8)

16. Military stronghold devastated the right forests (8)

17. Los Angeles daughter has a young man (3)

20. My reflection collected in her confused verse (5)

22. Garbled cue: pack small baked treat (7)

24. Surly among consul lenders (6)

25. Foul-smelling grade (4)

26. Unpleasant leaders left ancestral line (5)

Down

1. Example of maples in pieces (6)

2. Garden pest cruelly slain (5)

3. Loaned me cooked citrus drink (8)

4. Aussie bird's lemur has no fringes (3)

5. Beseech little devil over legends (7)

6. Exhaled on the air, depressed (4)

11. Beg for soft heavy metal (5)

12. Delay the German grasping the iron (5)

14. Some cuts wrecked the fancy outfits (8)

15. Trip over scattered elm tubs (7)

18. Enquiring about lazing in the sun, topless (6)

19. Hair-raising vehicle in the Seychelles! (5)

21. Take a handful, drop the centre, and pull (4)

23. Tavern invested in domain name (3)

Puzzle 20

Across

1. Sodium got on crumpled pink serviette (6)

4. Spatter quietly, 50 wrapped in a cloth band (6)

9. Mined the wrong way to get fabric (5)

10. Tail Ian, tottering from Rome, perhaps? (7)

11. Someone hides for a very long time (3)

12. Cruelly reject incentive before noon (5)

13. Gad obtains little devices (7)

15. Broke in on bizarre Runt Pet ride (11)

21. Ship's captain is one who hops about (7)

24. It's typical for us to join University Alabama (5)

25. Repair, without heading to the finish (3)

26. Australia, Turkey, and Iowa join to form a republic (7)

27. Chow down! It's boiled uranium paté! (3,2)

28. Elegant characters in double entendres system (6)

29. Strapping Romeo in home office (6)

Down

1. One who avoids clothes endlessly dusting all over the place (6)

2. Antarctic bird upending pie, excluding daughter (7)

3. 2,000 in turbulent Seine — it's huge! (7)

5. Spent, acquiring length of chequered cloth (5)

6. Nimble American soldier got into the beer! (5)

7. Shaken up, the son is truthful (6)

8. Cruelly gibed ranger making edible housing material? (11)

14. Belly held in by alarming utensil (3)

16. What's the point of the dump? (3)

17. Cautious prude went to the Northern Territory (7)

18. Queen got around busy quota line around the Earth (7)

19. Lively lads in the atoll (6)

20. Slapdash Papa in bungled ploys (6)

22. Explosive use is a problem (5)

23. Parish covers French city (5)

Puzzle 21

Across

1. Turns up distorted sepia film (9)
6. Give in to archery equipment (3)
8. Half note unaffected when played backwards (5)
9. Italian wine's from a chitin mixture (7)
10. Manoeuvre the bullock (5)
11. Cracked tan gems make lodestones (7)
13. Primates concealed by tapestry (4)
15. Settle with monsieur instead of soprano, it shows fortitude (6)
16. Altered a licit sloping font (6)
19. Mark's a scholar without heart (4)
21. Umbrella with ornate opals covering sun god (7)
24. Heavenly messenger removed edges of the tangelo (5)
25. Wildly moronic Greek letter (7)
26. Tenor with reckless rubbish (5)
28. It's the night before, either way (3)
29. Fiery bond forged with sweetheart (9)

Down

1. Line up piece of raiment (3)
2. Quiet United Nations gentleman has a strong smell (7)
3. Loony liar mom's unethical (7)
4. Frolicsome mice on wages (6)
5. Carol can consume whiskey, and sway (5)
6. Begin dreadful drinking bout (5)
7. Quaint and eccentric wish claim (9)
10. Busily share poem message with flags (9)
12. Continent that's part of quasi-alliance (4)
14. Peru note is also Mexican currency (4)
17. Turkey performer has a farm vehicle (7)
18. Kind of gauge 50 good suitcases (7)
20. Emotionally dependent fish in Cyprus (6)
22. Sounds like beams are set upright (5)
23. Credit in bus, going north to the bush (5)
27. Concealed sample of orchid (3)

Puzzle 22

Across

1. Shows off British scraps (5)
4. Cocktail infests health (7)
8. Admonish careless errand imp (9)
9. Tear fast current (3)
10. Pithy trees regenerated (5)
11. Guarantee note set in prose (7)
13. Grabs hold of Greek snakes! (6)
15. Hot drink dispenser ate top stew (6)
17. Special bi dudes are close friends (7)
18. Shriek, losing head, to get dairy product (5)
20. Computer game includes a work unit (3)
22. Insanely trot to India's historical convention (9)
23. Cause great suffering to scrappy cur's ego (7)
24. Rival Zulu left transmuted enzyme (5)

Down

1. Bereft without France's flat cap (5)
2. Demolished snared amp and sign (9)
3. Distilled wines for pigs (5)
4. Drink very quietly amidst mixed fare (6)
5. Pod at sea in story for a baby frog (7)
6. Make a mistake in part of Barrier Reef (3)
7. Somehow, a spinet is intelligent? (7)
12. Unpredictable epic miser is vague (9)
13. Inebriated, begs lot of wine glasses (7)
14. Suffering territory for artist (7)
16. Break free from El Salvador Cape (6)
18. The Italian found in Guevara's country (5)
19. Primate lost kilo of banknotes (5)
21. Slime is endlessly wonderful! (3)

Puzzle 23

Across

1. Interrupt improper rust bid (7)
5. Charlie, I recalled set quotes (5)
8. Horrify a quiet friend (5)
9. Submerge upsetting memories, missing Oscar (7)
10. Decapitation murders lead to problems! (4)
11. Elastic clip kits for make-up (8)
13. Accidentally drench darling offspring's offspring (13)
16. Elegant ecru flag flying (8)
17. Block the wooden shoe! (4)
20. Cooked up ma viper for Dracula, perhaps? (7)
21. Stressed verb form (5)
22. Cruel, corrupt money (5)
23. Gathered around retiring rani's mosque tower (7)

Down

1. Doctor has a wing illustration (7)
2. Make watertight around Portugal's flower part (5)
3. Hideous feature of smug lynx (4)
4. Submit mushier plastic home for the Rosetta Stone (7,6)
5. Hit mosaic with the French woman's top (8)
6. Retire rambling with Rex, a small dog (7)
7. Second vegetable is smooth and glossy (5)
12. Dave hies out to get glue (8)
14. Unsteady main ace doesn't have enough iron (7)
15. Disregard Charlie in gentle break up (7)
16. Grit scratched the right judge's hammer (5)
18. Lutetium, nitrogen and argon from the moon (5)
19. British school held by skeletons! (4)

Puzzle 24

Across

3. Big cat lost his first charged particle (3)

7. Papa has disgust for speaker's platform (6)

8. Steers clear of insanely sad Eve (6)

9. Perverse main son gets a stately home (7)

10. The French got into a car, it's obvious (5)

11. Parent's involved in propaganda drive (3)

12. Second-rate iron? Fire got out of hand! (8)

16. Rag cad in unravelled knitted top (8)

18. Spicy, even in throat! (3)

21. Begin street painting (5)

22. Mammal from Ireland involved in gaffe (7)

24. Undergarment sector is jittery (6)

25. Weird aliens' salt solution (6)

26. Young horse dropped 50 for baby bed (3)

Down

1. Composition of cooked oats got around North America (6)

2. Dynamically ski OK to sales hut (5)

3. I'm being a model, it's impressive! (8)

4. Sounds like was aware of novel (3)

5. Garment-makers' gold invested in tails (7)

6. Italian ice cream got ale mixture (6)

11. Informal medico brought back cod (3)

13. Crushing fine nuts is most amusing (8)

14. Rodent's regularly truant (3)

15. Present day frock's location (7)

17. Public sale without uniform deed (6)

19. Upset with rotten finish (6)

20. Backwards elf gets around sailor's moral tale (5)

23. Even in lettuce, and so on (3)

Puzzle 25

Across

1. Intricate piñata shows the lustre of age (6)

4. Creature from hectic Manila (6)

7. Cool road construction leads to American state (8)

8. Tropical tree's lamp broke (4)

9. Pole and dune grain (4)

11. Cairo inhabitant cooked a tangy pie (8)

13. Cruelly foul up users' surplus (11)

16. Grows smaller, sadly swindled (8)

19. Sound reflection in biotech office (4)

22. Leave with an unknown in a twisted tie (4)

23. Read aloud attendance to get gifts (8)

24. Grown-up mate got around old city (6)

25. Snoops about to get cutlery items! (6)

Down

1. Stows away cap back in Kansas (5)

2. Shaped tonal bird's claw (5)

3. Non-professional Asian involved in trauma treatment (7)

4. Suffering in the past, over New York (5)

5. Aim to get back to Michigan, from Florida's city (5)

6. Crushed melon fruit (5)

10. Sauce held by Oedipus (3)

12. Donkey and asps missing papa (3)

13. Noticed the hand tool (3)

14. Pays attention to intricate tinsels (7)

15. Unit came in first, from the sound of it (3)

16. Armed violent ambition (5)

17. Outer wrappings removed from edition, confused the halfwit! (5)

18. Break in concentration ruins leaps (5)

20. African river condo has golf for day (5)

21. Water hole foundation has nothing for British (5)

Chapter **4**
Challenging Cryptics

his chapter has a nice collection of medium-level cryptics. I've written these for those who feel more confident about solving cryptics, and would like a bit more of a challenge.

I've made them a little harder than the easy crosswords by using a broader vocabulary both in the grids and in the clues. Some definitions are a bit more oblique, and some abbreviations may be a bit harder. There are some words 'in plain view' within the clues (where you don't need to find a synonym), but not as many as in the easy crosswords in Chapter 3. There are also more anagram clues than you see in a regular cryptic, but fewer than in the easy crosswords.

Puzzle 26

Across

1. A radar cub mistakenly gets a predatory fish (9)
8. Go berserk, ignoring heart's fury (4)
9. Juliet has Asian old record identifying a rugged vehicle (4)
10. Smallest in the litter is partly disgruntled (4)
12. Artfully heed round German's green fence (5)
14. Thump around uniform for an Aussie great (5)
16. Glaze the circle evenly (3)
17. Gollum's cry on getting stirred rice soup (8)
20. Small combat vehicle smelled revolting (5)
21. Strangely say nil in Anglo-Saxon examination! (8)
22. Consume first cut of steak, for example (3)
23. Edgy bridge player very upset (5)
25. Rounded purple fruit put on piano (5)
28. Alpert's aromatic plant (4)
30. Diplomacy about messy attic I left (4)
31. Assistant's crazy idea (4)
32. Intermission until deer performs (9)

Down

2. Assert and rave madly (4)
3. Indian currency for blended purée (5)
4. Leads astray ill-bred port curs (8)
5. Ned returned to lair (3)
6. Whiskey, as well as a magic stick! (4)
7. Nicest yes altered prerequisite (9)
11. Stocky baby bird has short time for Charlie (5)
13. Unhappily repaid asp to get lost (9)
14. Gamble on a Greek letter (4)
15. Teach the entourage (5)
18. Letter to south-eastern doctor on the French musical group (8)
19. Accept orders from confused boy assimilating English (4)
20. Hush around layer going up to air spirit (5)
24. Temperature in vial is crucial (5)
26. Revoke United Nations party (4)
27. Sour advertisement got about 101 (4)
29. Very long time in a dungeon (3)

Puzzle 27

Across

1. Harmless credit notes contain nitrogen and no copper (9)
6. Lettuce is part of costume (3)
8. Slow tempo good in vocal backing (5)
9. Separate corrupted tea oils (7)
10. Yell 'Quiet out!' (5)
11. Dishevelled punk met drunk (7)
13. Escape from the Spanish bridge player (4)
15. Eaters' dynamic festival celebrating spring (6)
16. West Australia has teetotaller with the French acacia (6)
19. Connecticut included in Anglo-Saxon performances (4)
21. Busily ate long citrus fruit (7)
24. Carbon corrosion produces outer layer of loaf (5)
25. Own up to swindle on iron steamship (7)
26. Staff youngster devoured sweet (5)
28. 12 down's juvenile form is oddly effete (3)
29. Censure rum present in Senegal's beach lotion (9)

Down

1. Sickly Billy lost his covers (3)
2. Yes, Spanish left souvenirs all over the place, highly strung (7)
3. Laugh loudly; tenor and apprentice involved in drudgery! (7)
4. Repulsive, yet melodious? Scratch Mel! (6)
5. Wading bird coming from street, or Cambodia (5)
6. 150 intend to make an allegation (5)
7. Tamest ewe somehow gets a piece of confectionary (9)
10. Unexpectedly accepts the French pageant (9)
12. Changed temperature for small amphibian (4)
14. Spoken moral needs no introduction (4)
17. As civil engineer and tenor in charge are austere . . . (7)
18. Fretful about rare fungus (7)
20. Company American at home to relation (6)
22. No French alien has nine players (5)
23. Female sheep grabbing right water jugs (5)
27. Longing for Japanese money (3)

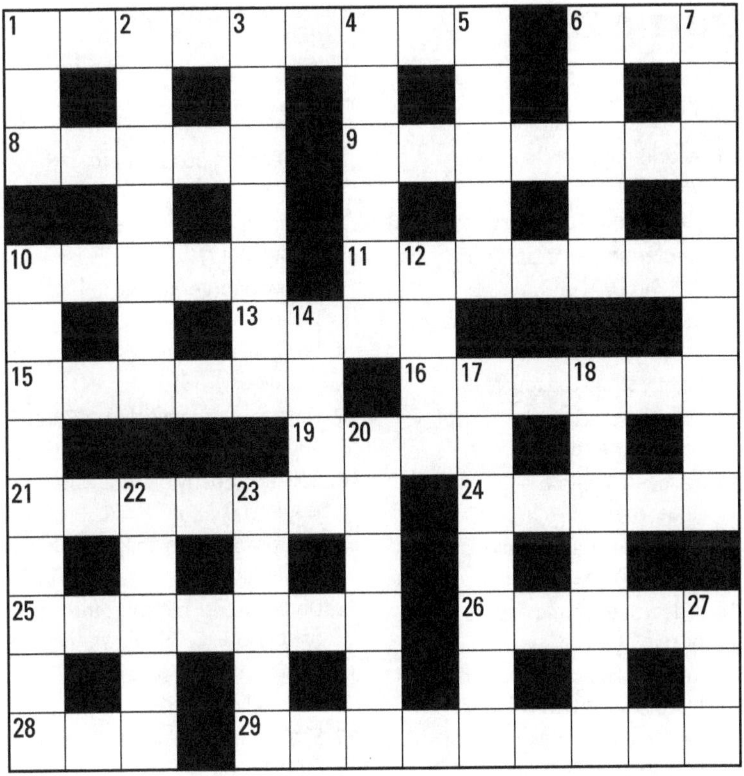

Puzzle 28

Across

1. Accidentally sprain Papa's vegetable (7)

5. Taxi! Queen tossed tree trunk! (5)

8. Deuterium left in spine of spinning rod (7)

9. Liquefies and mixes metals without an adult (5)

10. Lightly strike the faucet (3)

11. Wholehearted and surprisingly nicer in the south-east (7)

13. Three misused the anaesthetic (5)

14. Organised, halest clinics provide gymnastic exercises (13)

18. A dearth of an old expression of dismay? (5)

19. Remote Aussie region suffering blackout, without line (7)

23. Oddly, shogun has a former French coin (3)

24. Forbid Jo from supplying stringed instrument (5)

25. Ornate inset is for Michelangelo's ceiling (7)

26. Narrow hilltop reached via overpass, missing entrance (5)

27. Longed for 12 months with Ned (7)

Down

1. Is French in postscript to nuisances? (5)

2. Wear the crown — it sounds like a downpour! (5)

3. Elbow George, getting in unclothed (5)

4. Pompously pouts, entirely ridiculously (13)

5. Domestic animal got into 'Come and Battle' (7)

6. Ballet company oils hob, after a fashion (7)

7. Confused rosters for holiday destinations (7)

12. Unperturbed, cut short the unit of heat energy (3)

14. Church has honey-yellow assembly room (7)

15. Shakespearean king and Ned are scholarly (7)

16. Abysmally smokier and annoying (7)

17. Cannibal's holding a pen tip (3)

20. Perplexing Ascot Opera by Puccini (5)

21. Line up, with energy rather than gravity, to discover an extraterrestrial (5)

22. Reportedly, it's a requirement to work dough (5)

Puzzle 29

Across

1. Bubbly chap — nag me mischievously! (9)
8. Bath bar and duck stuck in plant's fluid (4)
9. Obscure promo text cut short (4)
10. Arsenic? Getting to grips with identification helps! (4)
12. Nasty Ox Tic is poisonous (5)
14. Curiously peevish without six rams (5)
16. Topless chicken's a nocturnal bird (3)
17. Unlucky number affected trite hen (8)
20. Street on East Boulder (5)
21. Bungled gin ratio for pasta tubes (8)
22. Vehicle is busier? Not half! (3)
23. Musical exercise's a complicated Asian duet (5)
25. The Spanish flipper's impish (5)
28. Announced one who adjusts the pitch of fish (4)
30. Victor England and Albert produce delicate meat (4)
31. Very small note to New York (4)
32. Commotion caused by weird ant noises (9)

Down

2. Possess the cargo space (4)
3. Demonstration month (5)
4. A mother otter turned up with almond liqueur (8)
5. Taken aback, Don gives signal (3)
6. Scam among macho axe-men (4)
7. Soprano quietly incises cooked curry quality (9)
11. Son ripped into retail outlet (5)
13. Cute ergot damaged zucchini (9)
14. Strike a garden pest! (4)
15. Ring from hotel, during open disturbance (5)
18. Somehow sail it in to get first letters (8)
19. European river Liberia bisects the English quarter (4)
20. Impede daring feat (5)
24. Four cutting Dot's bit of grass (5)
26. Keen on, yet frowned, oddly (4)
27. Town leader dismisses end to brief dressing (4)
29. Operate part of the carousel (3)

Puzzle 30

Across

2. Gallium put in beer and seaweeds (5)

7. Male bovine's stupid talk (4)

8. Don took a top class kilo of Japanese radish (6)

9. Paid no attention to dingo re mess (7)

10. Chinese mammal has forty winks on the way back with District Attorney (5)

12. Weep in crypt (3)

13. Oblivious to rating on cocktail (8)

16. My hat set off the gem (8)

17. Broadcaster's book set in ancient times (1,1,1)

20. Disdain for southern maize (5)

22. Conspire with devilish old clue (7)

24. Sadly, last seen in Church of England citadel (6)

25. University 10's operating system (4)

26. At home in the German railway carriage for food (5)

Down

1. Need to feed her gnu mash (6)

2. Associate gets a ring from metal mixture (5)

3. Ravenously messed up Grey Deli (8)

4. School's domain deduced, in part (3)

5. Offbeat brazier buckled (7)

6. Daring bishop advanced in years (4)

11. Prank went off? Can it! (5)

12. Outer garments and Ascot torn (5)

14. Building got inner gas (8)

15. Redo sample of meteorite rates (7)

18. Bud (American soldier) got Eastern Aussie parakeet (6)

19. Sounds like blossom yields powder (5)

21. Nail the carbon regulation (4)

23. Gave food to little Federal agent (3)

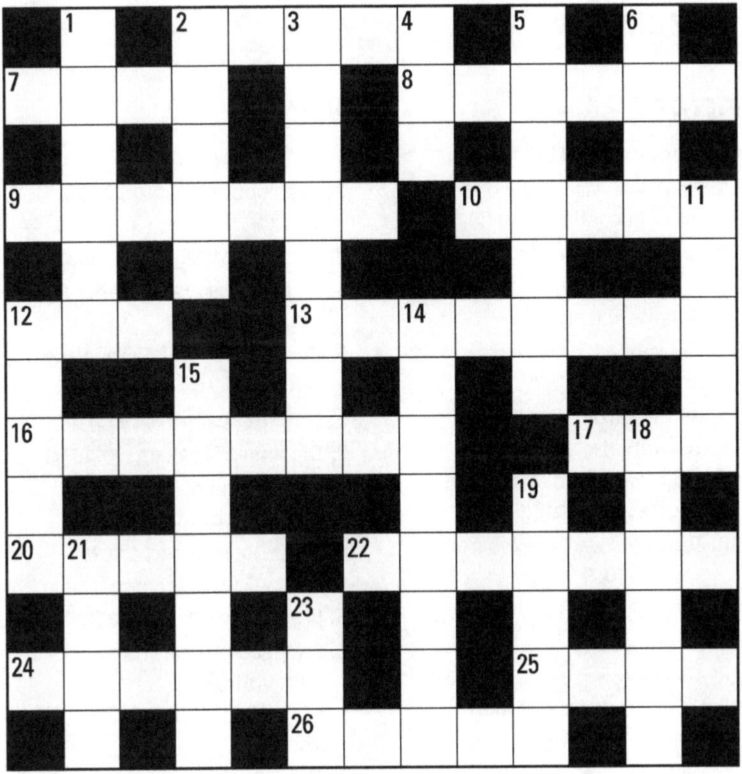

Puzzle 31

Across

1. Maniac cut nail badly (7)

5. Graduate has revolutionary kit to make decorated cloth (5)

8. Greek got sick from barbecue (5)

9. Nickel ring found in United Nations Alliance (5)

10. Flow out from the east, very black (3)

11. Betrayal from unstable senator (7)

13. From the sound of it, raised brioche, perhaps? (5)

14. Terry jabs warm mixed fruit spread (10,3)

17. Ransack quickly with a gun (5)

19. Scrutinise lively meanie holding a cross (7)

23. Drink slowly from siphon (3)

24. Twit goes around second bend (5)

25. I tucked into lard with Scottish landowner (5)

26. Singe with gas for bridge player's joint (5)

27. Replacement animal park (7)

Down

1. Lamp is not heavy (5)

2. Ingenuous citizen forgot the time (5)

3. Pitiless, reveals game pieces (5)

4. Anyhow, Pen, repay pence for hot spice! (7,6)

5. Burst bubble with Romeo and weep loudly (7)

6. Once more than once (5)

7. Dig monk! Break up realm! (7)

12. Exclamation of surprise concealed by Mata Hari (3)

14. Cross out incorrect charts covering Cuba (7)

15. Brawl and swelter dreadfully (7)

16. Sweet potato may come back up! (3)

18. Fake mixed gin has added iron (5)

20. Titan's book of maps (5)

21. Rice I blended is colder (5)

22. Provide with an ability to endure without Rex (5)

Puzzle 32

Across

1. Demur irregularly about company etiquette (7)
5. Polite four and I invested in Sri Lanka (5)
8. Go around cay with high tension boat (5)
9. Jawless fish destroyed my pearl (7)
10. Concerning a letter identifying the coral ridge . . . (4)
11. Great Lake is high-quality (8)
13. Shrewd; cooked precious aspic (13)
16. Special importance shown by the same deformed hips (8)
17. Unit of heredity obtained from Georgia on gas (4)
20. Attitude of private investigator tucking into onion (7)
21. Frighten Albert with a limb (5)
22. The Spanish echo Connecticut's vote (5)
23. Trifled with drunk bald Deb (7)

Down

1. Short journey hit pay dirt! (7)
2. Bike men avoid clemency, confused (5)
3. Announce draft ceremony (4)
4. Unfortunately, final document developed a fault (13)
5. Begin business with 1000 men and the Church of England (8)
6. Dizziness? Got it back in mysterious grove (7)
7. Hen's sheet (5)
12. Beekeeper Pa at iris, wandering around (8)
14. Peter, lurching around the Italian, is a cold-blooded one (7)
15. Yours truly got into stewed dates, cooked over hot water (7)
16. Wear down hesitation to poem (5)
18. Em has old trouble with computer communication (5)
19. Boast stuck up clothes (4)

Puzzle 33

Across

1. Trench map design on prepared animal skin (9)
8. Insult garden pest with Romeo, instead of George (4)
9. Carry vagrant who lost heart (4)
10. Adorable copper note (4)
12. I got out of disorganised unisex connection (5)
14. Short time with one ace radium diadem (5)
16. Cut off end from fruit and vegetable (3)
17. Stubborn about red cuckoo (8)
20. Tin ore can be noisy! (5)
21. Coin and tossed dice occur simultaneously (8)
22. Carmine's part of the fire department (3)
23. Point in easy whipped up article (5)
25. A good man with fish has a knife sharpener (5)
28. Food shop from French Long Island (4)
30. Five-in-one variety cooker! (4)
31. I got silver ring for Othello's foe (4)
32. Practical magic part is disguised (9)

Down

2. Top primate gets kiss (4)
3. Company rig confused short dog (5)
4. Pasta penguin (8)
5. Even insults Brazil, for example (3)
6. Fine slack textile (4)
7. Musical increase roughly censored, unexpectedly (9)
11. Result? Endures mix-up without doctor (5)
13. Astronaut's outfit has renovated tissue cap (9)
14. Cab's tariff number one (4)
15. Sailor gets doe at sea house (5)
18. Sauce for bandage (8)
19. Crooked feature of straw rye (4)
20. Burn carbon and aluminium in South Dakota (5)
24. Abloom, hear odd Hawaiian greeting (5)
26. Therefore, ogre climbed up (4)
27. So far, I revealed the snowman (4)
29. Lost initial horror of organ (3)

Puzzle 34

Across

3. Bellows, right on Avenue Sierra! (5)

7. Secure accident, and get out of danger (6)

8. Moment at castle ditch (4)

9. Take into custody in Arkansas and take a break (6)

10. Prize hypocrite goes nuts without ice (6)

11. Harbour fortified wine (4)

12. Frantically urge halt to chortling (8)

15. Roughly mop score for Mozart, for instance (8)

18. Stadium lost north region (4)

19. Throws out damaged goods, without capital (6)

21. Serves jaunty poems (6)

23. Mace Melange is the high point (4)

24. Legally responsible for rejecting bail to the French (6)

25. Potassium in busy ants' containers (5)

Down

1. Precious diamond on ear (4)

2. Receive carbon copy discovered in bungled tape (6)

3. Sets lyre off, and designs again (8)

4. Animal doctor wears small waistcoat (4)

5. Clean-shaven male in new shoot (6)

6. Du Maurier's shrub (6)

9. Air conditioning around southern Greek character with savoury jelly (5)

13. Undoes knitting for Ravel in blazing sun (8)

14. Wanders thoroughfares with master, instead of daughter (5)

16. Protest against the thingamajig (6)

17. Help oneself to shaken Coke in the midst of exercise (6)

18. A woman overseas (6)

20. Stupefy with upside down nuts (4)

22. El Salvador brought in the Spanish long fish (4)

Puzzle 35

Across

1. Flying mammal at hotel, but went back to soaking place (7)
5. Unhitch drunk, lost in bunny home (5)
8. Who in France gets into old records supply? (5)
9. Mildew mound gets left for bridge player (5)
10. Sick doctor dropped out from training exercise (3)
11. Wild petrel, around Zambia, got a salty snack (7)
13. Ball game confused Greek character (5)
14. Have a less important role, and insanely abate cake task (4,1,4,4)
17. Middle Earth peoples' victor got stuck into flailing eels (5)
19. Took on perplexed dad poet (7)
23. Old boy and I got a sash (3)
24. Christmas song from a queen in Colorado (5)
25. Herald's abysmal ire disrupting credit (5)
26. Point 11 at the French refugee (5)
27. Printing mistake from maturer composition (7)

Down

1. Bass with rind jumps up to make an electronic noise (5)
2. Cuba involved in genuine ceasefire (5)
3. Gem pot sent back to Arizona (5)
4. Beau sails? Boil mixed fish stew! (13)
5. Turned edge to catch poisonous plant (7)
6. Grey strip goes around uniform (5)
7. Northern Territory comes after snake monster with a fireman's pipe (7)
12. Draw neckwear (3)
14. Tellurium wrapped around mixed clear syrup (7)
15. Acquit sailor, and answer (7)
16. Sarsaparilla contains juice (3)
18. Flustered, drive to opera composer (5)
20. Exist and concur, strangely missing the point (5)
21. Contaminate artificial intelligence involved in explosive (5)
22. Wheat from the French has rum (5)

Puzzle 36

Across

1. Flustered, rushes escorts (6)
4. Dried grape is in downpour (6)
7. Swallows one's scum, unfortunately (8)
8. Initially, Ingrid overcomes worst anxious state (4)
9. Stop up and gulp back (4)
11. Sprinted with hessian bags to raids (8)
13. Engineer stationed in terminus (11)
16. Dipped in liquid, and simmered roughly (8)
19. A fruit, I've heard, produces two of a kind (4)
22. Small bit of land's getting into paisley (4)
23. Public relations with bad poetry effects (8)
24. Hot spice is good during deviant reign (6)
25. Nomads crush plum (6)

Down

1. Remove lid and clean-up afresh, leaving out the French (5)
2. Back to uniform for follower of Brahma (5)
3. Japanese nobleman confused Maria and us (7)
4. Sloppily rinse the pine sap (5)
5. Uncomplaining, I get into overturned baby beds (5)
6. Approaches broken snare (5)
10. Air-like substance can sink down the wrong way (3)
12. Family can be endlessly warm-hearted (3)
13. Block mother sheep (3)
14. Robot's mysterious iron dad (7)
15. Little devil only half contaminated (3)
16. Rejoicing, holds cake topping! (5)
17. The Spanish get into Monday's fruit (5)
18. Excellent fancy purse (5)
20. Races around units of land (5)
21. Egg in yarn damaged the fibre (5)

Puzzle 37

Across

1. Dot leaves the outlandish Democrats, and beats butter and sugar (6)
4. Present day breach off course (6)
9. Newton covered by Visa account (5)
10. Ma Cuba and little Elizabeth, from the Scottish play (7)
11. The Australian Labor Party initially found on a mountain (3)
12. Scramble up branch after Charlie (5)
13. Pragmatist's genuine first (7)
15. Cross-examined and reviewed nit sloppily (11)
21. Irritated truant with Mike's fit of rage (7)
24. Stroll to doctor tucking into beer (5)
25. Aussie runner found among the chrysanthemums (3)
26. Medical course for army unit is endless (7)
27. Smallest slate broke (5)
28. Frankfurter from riotous to-do, set in Mercury! (3,3)
29. Take part in a teetotal resolution (6)

Down

1. Secure 150 in Switzerland (6)
2. Joy from broken toe-nail! (7)
3. Gruesome mare acquires taxi (7)
5. Russian cottage's agile arachnid ignored Rin (5)
6. Boudicca's tribe has frozen water and nickel (5)
7. South Pacific island's back-to-front hat? It has one (6)
8. Novel *Venom Permit* is a change for the better (11)
14. Short cow's sound (3)
16. Odd trout for a young child (3)
17. Paul, in tee, turned over decoration on an American uniform (7)
18. Hug and point to masculine British ace (7)
19. Organised charts for collar stiffener (6)
20. Ocean Ted settled on a chair (6)
22. Dark, outspoken chevalier (5)
23. Messy room contains echo of Juliet's love (5)

Puzzle 38

Across

2. Live coal dropped off head of subscriber! (5)

7. Ship's stabiliser knocked over vegetable (4)

8. Learnt about deer's horn (6)

9. Spice vehicle at a distance (7)

10. Falsify the buttery sweet (5)

12. Hardly any point to go after iron (3)

13. Dine, drunk, with Penny? It's obscene! (8)

16. I got into unruly debates identifying disease (8)

17. Glass pot comes from Japan and Arkansas (3)

20. Goes out with dried fruits (5)

22. Abstinent cat ices soup (7)

24. Excavate broken-down hovels (6)

25. Sea-eagle found in the wilderness (4)

26. Wall art from ancient city in Malaysia (5)

Down

1. Scold angrily about incorrect rebate (6)

2. Pompous composer's rising fury about student (5)

3. Plant specialist tints boa strangely (8)

4. Evenly arrange old cloth (3)

5. Stalwart one in Paris, with Charlie, gets into turned up hats (7)

6. British energy unit represents little ice mass (4)

11. Tenant lost introduction to cross the threshold (5)

12. Note, daughter, Edward's washed out! (5)

14. Outlandishly stares after Diana? Catastrophe! (8)

15. Watch old boy perform duties (7)

18. Foreigners whisk up saline (6)

19. It's flat and smooth in both directions (5)

21. Pallid hay's destroyed (4)

23. Confused male lost a tree (3)

Puzzle 39

Across

1. Ed went back on Monday to the fiend (5)

4. Washington peak is wetter (7)

8. Laughs at jumbled lurid ices (9)

9. Goddess of the dawn features in theosophy (3)

10. Reprocess, heads off with bike (5)

11. Sensitive accidental fault got around Connecticut (7)

13. North American country can get a District Attorney (6)

15. The Seychelles and Switzerland get stuck into Peru's spirit (6)

17. Melodious university involved in artful claims (7)

18. Decorate with radon freely (5)

20. Time in therapy (3)

22. Disclosure from ad assignment (9)

23. Hang up pen inside the beaten suds (7)

24. Savoury turnover is wan (5)

Down

1. Orchid arrangement ignored hotel's style of architecture (5)

2. Snide mice fabricated drugs (9)

3. Husband in pleasant alcove (5)

4. Recount revolutionary tale in note (6)

5. Six-footers are in cults! (7)

6. Anger among vampires (3)

7. Sort it out, and do this clue again! (7)

12. Café riots damage manufacturing complexes! (9)

13. Those in tents scamper awkwardly (7)

14. Read out thanks in new edict (7)

16. Chaotic bedlam held responsible (6)

18. A broken peso for the Greek storyteller (5)

19. Carer from North America's northern New York (5)

21. Broadsheet contains promotions (3)

Puzzle 40

Across

3. Romeo got out of crustacean's taxi (3)

7. Retain damaged part of the eye (6)

8. Rail at incorrect lasso (6)

9. Face up to a horrible task, and cruelly tilt beetle hub (4,3,6)

10. Dial tone employed by singer (4)

11. Appreciating Jenny, I go nuts (8)

14. Most delicate bustle went to pieces in the street (8)

16. The Terrible Name (4)

18. Drummer's version inspires scout (13)

20. George and the Queen meet a guy from Köln (6)

21. Plague horrible bosses (6)

22. Understanding of Barbie's partner (3)

Down

1. Affable Georgia reclined back (6)

2. Fetch in boom, to wrong tool for a thorough search? (4-5,4)

3. Complex mesh used in care of goat's wool (8)

4. Little Robert has left a blotch (4)

5. Hastily ignore insane dental assistant! (4,9)

6. Little seabird seen around Avenue Inn (6)

10. Even sambas reveal abdominal muscles (3)

12. Chuck off Juliet and alien with titanium son (8)

13. German not out of spirit (3)

15. Irregular United Nations gets Eve to Norway (6)

17. Help donkey get first (6)

19. Submerged skunk lost a kilo (4)

Puzzle 41

Across

1. Plant explodes! Ba boom! (6)
4. Ranges of different copses (6)
9. It's an article of faith, whichever way you look at it (5)
10. Desperate salesmen lost 50, all at once (2,5)
11. Every one of the banks left the demonstration (3)
12. The French rum tipped over the primate (5)
13. Got no toes? Sounds like it, sugar! (7)
15. Hard work to mistakenly erase web log (5,6)
21. Quieter festival acquiring new tellurium (7)
24. Flyer's physical training includes fishy oil (5)
25. Contemplate needle's gap (3)
26. A formal speech? Rain, too? Awful! (7)
27. Sounding out French resort for young relative (5)
28. Note Asian tenor — he cut gnashers (6)
29. Seven players performing Tempest, without Mike (6)

Down

1. Teetotaller found inside tree trunk with a flask! (6)
2. Very little half note to Albert (7)
3. 26 across at sea to Canadian province (7)
5. Hilarious business gets medium integrated circuit (5)
6. Poets stirred the basil sauce (5)
7. Cooked slowly for short time in mixed weeds (6)
8. Unstable teller being aggressive (11)
14. Hot drink bottled by anteater (3)
16. Prohibit hold up — catch in the act! (3)
17. Payment for British flower includes pens (7)
18. Entails bananas, it's important (7)
19. Very loud during rote translation attempt (6)
20. Confirm at exam (6)
22. Furious, I evaluate (5)
23. Tango with tall leg part (5)

Puzzle 42

Across

1. Divest of old records during car journey (7)

5. A principal in the future (5)

8. Sir Francis is rasher (5)

9. Bizarrely retrain the landscape (7)

10. Skating place forgot initial beverage (4)

11. Guard the special girl (8)

13. Unreasonably picky, editing lyric pie chart (13)

16. Damn epic, dreadful, widespread disease (8)

17. Concept from French in Iowa (4)

20. At home with Queen? Note answer's dullness (7)

21. Slid around violently, turned back to husband from Cardiff (5)

22. Intricately pleat part of flower (5)

23. More delicious, that is, in rummy cocktail (7)

Down

1. Blondie singer had robe buckled (7)

2. Gym got tin for nut (5)

3. Male children get iodine instead of sulphur's charged particles (4)

4. Doctor — order anti-x-ray, it's astonishing! (13)

5. Do away with manic Rob, breaking agate (8)

6. Shape the laciest stretchy band (7)

7. Benefactor Newton gets in the entrance (5)

12. Chinese, perhaps, can get the lie of the land with Albert (8)

14. Biting gentleman after a clever play on words (7)

15. The tanned hide vitamin in sudsy foam (7)

16. Preen and rip correct member of parliament (5)

18. Citadel history reveals an Indian city (5)

19. South-western instant message: 'Take a dip!' (4)

Puzzle 43

Across

1. Eve's ugly scars cause rifts (9)
6. Duck in company makes a dove's noise (3)
8. Lithograph of Romeo filling two US cups (5)
9. Crumbly castle? One in fable (7)
10. Jumped over grassy area before physical training (5)
11. Busy raid worker is joyful (7)
13. Exist around wickedness (4)
15. Stick fast to dubious header (6)
16. Knitted blanket from Kabul (6)
19. Tenor has one French melody (4)
21. Disown a musical group, performing (7)
24. Lemony sulphur pastries (5)
25. Worry and erupt violently with Rex Bravo (7)
26. Makes owl sounds? Shoot, sort of! (5)
28. Have a topless elegant dress (3)
29. Arrest Sue — criminal leads to valuables! (9)

Down

1. He left inexpensive hat (3)
2. Tomb inscription: 'Happiest, strangely, missing the point' (7)
3. Shrewder to manipulate stature (7)
4. Salvation Army bungled fair wildlife tour (6)
5. Kept an eye on curious bipeds, without a follower (5)
6. Sun god after a bit of corn for snake (5)
7. Unexpected Señor veto has connotations (9)
10. Oh! Alas! Spa treatment for long-haired dog! (5,4)
12. *Jonathan Creek* star is the Italian in Angola (4)
14. Animal doctor Oscar's absolute rejection (4)
17. Goes and gets complicated chef set (7)
18. Hard women's supporter comes up to our marina (7)
20. Ineffectual anomalous nebula (6)
22. Professional, in article, makes kitchen garment (5)
23. Demoralise democratic female relation (5)
27. Ring in ship's distress code (1,1,1)

Chapter **5**

Treacherous Cryptics

I n this chapter I present you with a collection of 'no holds barred' cryptic crosswords. These have normal sized grids, and occasionally stray into more difficult vocabulary.

These puzzles have fewer anagram clues, and use a wider range of abbreviations.

Check the reference lists in Chapter 2 if you're stuck, as the hard abbreviations and more unusual anagram indicators used in this chapter are included there.

Puzzle 44

Across

1. Bounding mammal locks, by the sound of it (4)
6. Oberon's knave provides ice hockey disc (4)
9. Choose the French relish (7)
11. Egyptian capital's air injected into gas (5)
12. Carroll's heroine has adult parasites (5)
13. Ivory Coast at back of the Italian fortress (7)
14. Many engaged in quiet lethargy (5)
16. Curiously normal, missing first tooth (5)
18. Victor bisecting hammered nail on blacksmith's block (5)
20. Fish gets one German vitamin and analgesic (7)
22. Ran back to evaluate verbal account (7)
24. More washed out doctor represents Sicilian capital (7)
26. Insanely himself? He's from Brussels! (7)
27. Bert's buddy comes from a Great Lake outside Norway (5)
28. Treasure commercial ore (5)
31. Force put in danger with check for weapons (5)
34. Excavate it, Capone, it's not analogue (7)
35. Hindu monk did backstroke, for example, to India (5)
36. Arsenic gets in, yet produces bread raiser (5)
37. Care of medium pot with English poached fruit (7)
38. Seasoning for sailor (4)
39. Regretted some of untrue diatribe (4)

Down

2. A note to go to Spanish friend (5)
3. Manage going back to Hungary's era (5)
4. Polish remover is very good added to pitch (7)
5. Albert, join in the boy with a lamp (7)
6. Sacred song affected the lamps (5)
7. Celsius elevation to freeze? (5)
8. Lays the blame, missing middle high cards (4)
10. Cut short strange low dam (4)
15. Tear old jazzy dancer's outfit (7)
17. Creative experts in desperate straits (7)
18. Accompaniment piece for Japanese cartoon (5)
19. A boy has the French soup server (5)

21. You called out to sheep (3)

23. Slam into wreck, reversing (3)

25. Gold magi returned with yours truly, showing paper art (7)

26. Discord, missing queen's stories (7)

28. Primate getting around southern church recess (4)

29. Criminal koalas left out of Japanese port (5)

30. Correct text about Cuba's official proclamation (5)

31. Air passenger's pamphlet (5)

32. Ludicrous canine lost his head and went to pieces (5)

33. Alternatively, knit them a wind-borne toy (4)

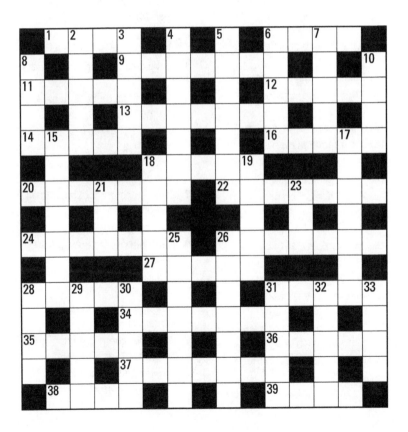

Puzzle 45

Across

1. Male poem to fashion (4)

3. The Thing lay off European country (5)

6. Irregular exams are leaderless for Christmas (4)

11. Crooned short tune backwards, to get a Spanish drink (7)

12. Left ante with qualified nurse's lamp (7)

13. Desiccated and tiresome (3)

14. Bitter leaves are randomly veined (6)

15. Loaned the Italian legume (6)

16. Use a spade to even edging (3)

18. Wrinkle new flaxen cloth (5)

20. Float high in the air (5)

22. Amelia's attention to hotel art (7)

23. Donate money for conclusion to expression of pain (5)

25. Compel politician to get into floral garland, in retirement (5)

28. Very well, tints cut at first (3)

29. Vulture Rod went back after Con (6)

30. Volcanic rock formed by barium with sodium chloride (6)

31. There's a fuss, even in the sand-box (3)

33. Bright red clarets mixed up (7)

34. Asian teetotaller breaking pale artist's board (7)

35. Wine is harmless, with potassium instead of fluorine (4)

36. I can get into twisted elms, and grin (5)

37. Depend upon answer lacking heart (4)

Down

1. Game error? Is diamond found in meal? (7)

2. New Zealand port's sand bank commotion (7)

4. Amphibian has toes, I've heard (4)

5. Flower is vigorous without centre (4)

7. Conductor's whirlpool ripped off 50 metres (7)

8. Undershirt torn? Glisten! (7)

9. Wow! Verbal nerd edited Huxley novel (5,3,5)

10. Tireless, yet failing debate badly (13)

16. Daughter gets complex, racy Austen heartthrob (5)

17. Minimalist composer has transparent substance (5)

19. Admirer gets iodine for fine swimmer, Thorpe (3)

21. Opponent sounds false (3)
23. Bridge player has 90 applications and defences (7)
24. Degree letter sent to Mark's country (7)
26. Blather quietly with baby's toy (7)
27. Sweepstake batch on terrace with Yankee (7)
31. Smallest piece found in anatomy? (4)
32. Gem ring next to friend (4)

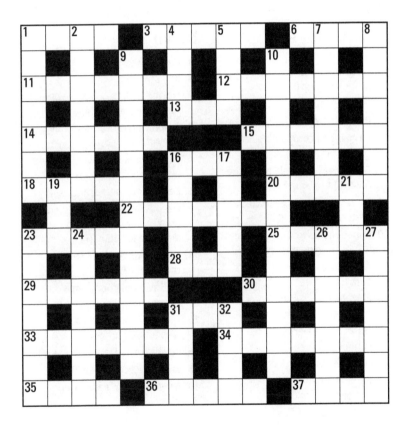

Puzzle 46

Across

1. Vague man's indebted arrangement (6-6)
7. Set fire to abandoned first vase (3)
9. Georgian place at lake has worker area (7)
11. Uncovered broken rosary part around Regina (5)
12. Greenish duck (4)
13. Resort to tree (5)
14. Embargo encompassing English coffee, maybe? (4)
17. Oddly neat snail relating to the nose (5)
18. Fantastic niece's boa makes a gesture of respect (9)
20. Impediments from old boy and felines running back to Les (9)
22. Alternative section of planet's path (5)
24. Introduction missing from reluctant sworn statement (4)
25. Upset about German submarine! (1-4)
27. Help with one Verdi opera (4)
30. Remove weapons from United Nations branch (5)
31. Missiles with parking, instead of resistance clothing features (7)
33. Meat's bad, actor! (3)
34. Rogue prison peahen causes trepidation (12)

Down

1. Canberra's area to take the initiative (3)
2. North America is after an edition for Dame Everage (4)
3. Amphibian ransacks, climbing up mushroom (9)
4. Permeate with sublime mixture (without quarter litre) (5)
5. Dash about with a missile (4)
6. Deep resentment expressed in underground prison with diamond for point (7)
8. Extinct humans' earthen lands changed (12)
9. Sir David bought ornate cuckoo (12)
10. Tilts over and acquires skills, without resistance (5)
15. Wash crushed lace with gas (5)
16. British racecourse tie (5)
19. A piece of cake eases a yip upset (4,2,3)

21. Settled on cost with a tangerine (7)

23. Salty water and soft French cheese coating pole (5)

26. Incendiary device added to eastern dessert! (5)

28. Husband gets Arabic piano instrument (4)

29. Decorates a cake with faults — no top! (4)

32. Evenly strewn number (3)

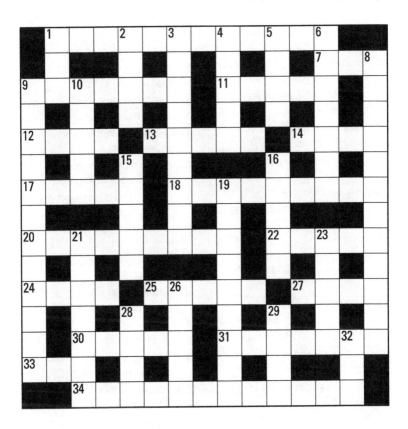

Puzzle 47

Across

3. Even middleman has a notion! (4)

5. Very quiet in the straw, content (5)

8. Slacken Liberal noose, after a fashion (6)

10. Apologetic, coming from street in Paris with bad flu (6)

11. Dodgy foreign bod shows fearful apprehension (10)

13. Crazy sniper mom provides fruit (9)

17. Therefore, go back to get monster (4)

20. Paddle mohair regularly (3)

21. Molten rock from Los Angeles and Virginia (4)

22. Sir returns in the afternoon for a triangular glass (5)

23. Give silver to artist at Taj Mahal site (4)

24. Indict university during quarter (3)

25. Spear wheeling animals (4)

27. Shifty archer yet to reveal perfidy (9)

31. Goals I've got: breaking things (10)

34. Motorway 51 to European Union environs (6)

35. Rank temperature (6)

36. Southern border of papyrus, for example (5)

37. Vegetable acceptable to sun god (4)

Down

1. Point after 150 foot fissure (5)

2. Rough sounding, like a stallion, I hear (6)

3. Irregular ion around fluorine led to little data (4)

4. Auntie befuddled without an old needle case (4)

6. Ameli to make a speech, and make things better (10)

7. Poor person's broadsheet got around Uruguay (6)

9. Comfortably-designed nice groom's puzzled (9)

12. Grow faint? I am after a vitamin (3)

14. Restoring confidence for us in new earrings (10)

15. Unbalanced pious mute is impulsive (9)

16. According to hearsay, a complex network produces corn (5)

18. Freelancer shows flair and enthusiasm (4)

19. Lawyer sailor let the cat out of the bag (4)

26. Albert gets tree from high mountains (6)

28. Removed head from light beer (3)

29. Return to note on French green (6)

30. Crooked Anglo-Saxon went to the Royal Botanical Gardens (5)

32. Yes, in German club with king and knave (4)

33. Fish has alto's last part of composition (4)

Puzzle 48

Across

1. Intoxicated crackpot jailer is a prankster (9,5)

9. Obstreperous coach pony makes a horrible racket (9)

10. Thailand gets approval for gecko (5)

11. Surround restless clones with energy (7)

13. Brisk papa involved in assault (5)

15. Dismissed beginner, and wrote parrot-fashion (4)

17. How women in America are widely known? (7)

19. Passes English slip-ups (7)

21. Pa returns during delay, changed to 29 February (4,3)

23. Blockade worker outside? Yes — in Spain, for example! (7)

25. Put together bomb's device (4)

26. The lady will get a conch, perhaps? (5)

28. Account goes to wading bird in underworld river (7)

29. Feminine hideaway's style (5)

31. New rebel alto is fairly good (9)

33. Get the whole gang to work from defective second dank hall (3,5,2,4)

Down

1. Canon in D composer's cheap bell is broken (9)

2. Bit of a circle contained in research (3)

3. Crept through the tulips? (7)

4. Coquettish around fine queen's food preparation (7)

5. So far, found in tardy baby's clothing (7)

6. Mammal's ceramics lost edges (5)

7. The Spanish king's moose (3)

8. Daughter gets unknown edition coloured (4)

12. Guevara gets around vocal sacred work (7)

14. French scientist's history on back street in Paris (7)

16. The Spanish exist for European flower (4)

18. Waste time with bread (4)

20. *The Grapes of Wrath* author's a bachelor wearing assorted neckties (9)

22. Batty aunty gets around California and Mexican state (7)

23. Hounds second-class birds of prey (7)

24. Has got back to ace, sprinted from the biggest desert (7)

26. Sieve fits poorly (4)

27. Mischievous, after left conifer (5)

30. Tool found on catwalk, even (3)

32. Insect sounds like a follower (3)

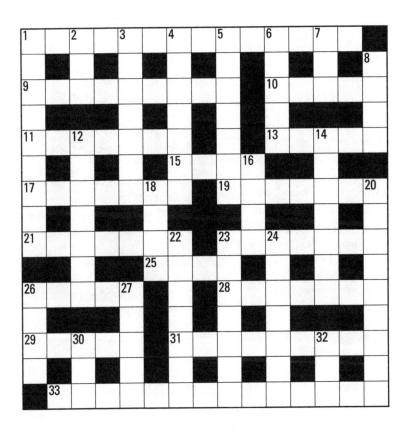

Puzzle 49

Across

1. Drag oneself along, inexperienced in Sri Lanka (5)

4. American Indian coachmen adapted (8)

9. Starry Little Bear roams ruin complex (4,5)

10. Jolly fellow from Pole gets a northern thank you (5)

11. Apropos in caption (3)

12. Intro to blended rich Italian ice cream (7)

13. Long Island Doctor's branch (4)

14. Twice carry out extinct bird (4)

16. Melanie and Ange's mixture (7)

18. Cumbersome work involved in honour (7)

20. State Jambalaya cooked without Juliet or Yankee (7)

23. Appreciates present day swamps (7)

25. Retreats are very black in El Salvador (4)

26. Short time to embrace hooligan (4)

28. Wicked light sources (7)

30. German letter set (3)

31. American state's chief declared (5)

32. Crushed remnant amid very large knick-knacks (9)

33. Uninterrupted, the French get into baffled masses (8)

34. Maine descendant's particle (5)

Down

1. Add the nobleman (5)

2. Land down under's Alcoholics Anonymous embraces odd rituals (9)

3. Poke fun at American diver about amplifier (7)

4. Tell all to remarkably fine doc (7)

5. Perverted drama in Uranus' satellite (7)

6. Retreat capital of Nepal is French (4)

7. Vietnamese capital's Chinese dynasty has ocean unit (5)

8. Caribbean island's scholar gets Botswana soda tipped over (8)

13. Bill has endless inadequacies (3)

15. Pulled car without front, and was in debt (4)

16. Yours truly and Alan let out; served up dinner, perhaps? (8)

17. Brave Georgia is with me (4)

19. Pal is near fantastic flying machines (9)

21. That is, leaving fawn's request (3)

22. Sailor, unaided, gets a tasty mollusc (7)

23. Climbs up a pole roughly to stumps (7)

24. Smallest mother goes after miniature (7)

27. The thing's collected by one French ally (5)

29. Lazy woman spins around? (5)

30. Microbe right inside jewel (4)

Puzzle 50

Across

1. Unscrupulous doggy gets vitamin for George (5)
4. Tin half of melodious finch (3)
6. Roasting at the Spanish traveller's establishment (5)
9. Stylish Kenneth's fowl (7)
10. Erin absolutely gets to Greek Furies (7)
11. Khan designed symbol of life (4)
12. Monster tenor to rotate (5)
13. Paragon has a silver deer (4)
16. Demonstration in Public Record Office exam (7)
18. Aria about scoundrel Pan's home (7)
20. British police devilishly bold and sick (3,4)
21. Doctor should produce a dry spell (7)
23. Six have this French perversion (4)
25. Italian children unknown, and need to scratch (5)
26. Street printer's measure leads to plant part (4)
30. Rice found in hectic barrio by the ocean (7)
31. Gourmet cocktail recipe includes uranium! (7)
32. Dadist is in Paris, embracing nurse (5)
33. Regularly scald — miserable (3)
34. Husband has a little routine (5)

Down

1. Champion following of the French surrealist (7)
2. Imbibe a dram of pen liquid (5)
3. Hitch up short country bumpkin (4)
4. Best wishes on giddily saluting actor! (15)
5. Insanely darned the leaden sewer's equipment (6,3,6)
6. What we breathe audibly, next in line (4)
7. Romantic meeting with translator in messy sty! (5)
8. Cooked analgesia, without, that is, an Italian dish in America (7)
14. 51 in hexadecimal coil (5)
15. Component without loud thespian (5)
17. Kimberley's banker even toured (3)
19. Hound the hound (3)
20. Get rid of it, above complex (7)

22. Shakespeare's last storm (7)

24. Driver's compartment in stateroom (5)

27. Hut fractured doctor's digit (5)

28. Brazil and Utah are very dry (4)

29. Top greeting next to Ghana (4)

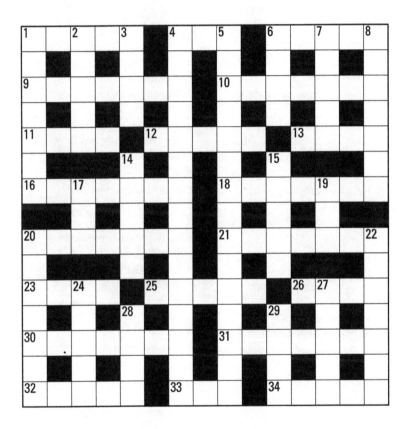

Puzzle 51

Across

1. Skinflint is in French sea (5)

4. Skirt seen on two Tuesdays (4)

6. Mother gets the Italian post (4)

10. Wellington Lake, for example, is unauthorised (7)

11. Tempted to cite badly, in the end (7)

12. Policemen go back around chaotic raid, it's irregular! (8)

14. Bring to mind Eve, retaining approval (5)

16. Naughty beetle, pay us for prettifying snooze! (6,5)

18. Chop down with Yankee, in place of hard conifer (3)

20. Squabble cut short in health resort (3)

22. Expert judge curses onion soup (11)

24. King and I infiltrate Poland, leading to immediate danger! (5)

25. *Dirty Harry* actor comes from the oriental forest (8)

28. Stalemate — I am out of date (7)

29. Merry four involved in lively fêtes (7)

30. Tough girls lost central playthings (4)

31. Tail end tenor aboard bus going in reverse (4)

32. Misbehaving cougars forget company, and get something sweet (5)

Down

1. Crowds bishop in between months (4)

2. Dished out weapons to get mangetout (4,3)

3. Head of state from Uruguay (and the French) rides in the Rolls Royce (5)

4. Wrench is evenly strung (3)

5. Sadly, our cheaters are perfidious (11)

7. Chief has nothing against getting into any preserved fish (7)

8. Guided Georgia to the shelf (5)

9. A tango entices — gives it a whirl! (8)

13. Impartiality is trendiest, somehow (11)

15. Wading bird heads off legal defences (4)

17. Inconsiderate thanks to Connecticut, with not as much (8)

19. Heat up tungsten appendage (4)

21. Shrivel up an ace prize cup (7)

23. Crumbling damage ignored (7)

24. Important fact: platinum captures active ion (5)

26. Insects looked back to postscript (5)

27. Shred eye drop (4)

29. Invent a story arc out of new fabric (3)

Puzzle 52

Across

1. Animosity to little rodents astride Albert (6)

4. Advertisement involved in escape adventure (8)

10. Fresh ice ran out for liqueur (9)

11. Snap up aerobic sample of immature insects (5)

12. Recline, with a piece of fiction (3)

13. Kindly father dotes liberally (4-7)

15. Demented geriatrics don't have Ire of the Stomach (7)

17. Expose academic occupying sunk wreck (6)

19. Taiwan's capital note about first class exercise (6)

20. Tenor — finish, right at the Italian vine's support (7)

22. Liberal cleanest inn's 100th anniversaries (11)

23. Costume conceals belly (3)

24. Gang of eight hug Connecticut alien (5)

26. I am with it, wearing scars from Eastern swords (9)

27. Subside frenzy around right to pay out funds (8)

28. Settled on silver marsh grass (6)

Down

1. Mushroom field's gloomy with unknown carbon mixture (8)

2. I got stuck into legends from French river (5)

3. Attach ropes incorrectly — disaster! (11)

5. I assault author insanely in Adelaide's state (5,9)

6. Viper's sudden intake of breath initially lost (3)

7. A very quiet place around the Queen's first course (9)

8. Corrects letter epilogues (6)

9. Purists often stir spice mixtures (14)

14. Berating awful ma hiding son (11)

16. Nate's after a deer that stands still (9)

18. Peeped at George with extraordinary dimples (8)

21. Air conditioning cable agreement (6)

23. Traffic art back to Delaware (5)

25. Greek letter regularly found inside teacup (3)

Puzzle 53

Across

3. The French added to Common Era tatting (4)

5. Adult maize nut (5)

8. Audibly scratches part of sentence (6)

10. Hang on to bridle restraining tenor and alto! (6)

11. Despicable sort of snowman (10)

13. Rolled tortilla left in hacienda accidentally (9)

17. Gestures to contrary son pinching daughter (4)

20. Hothead hides article (3)

21. Nurse tackles artificial intelligence in shower (4)

22. All the rage to be in post office snapshot (5)

23. Benin's after the Spanish woman (4)

24. Blaze misses finale for Christmas tree, for instance (3)

25. Sliced top off native American's tent with a fencing blade (4)

27. Bewilder old boy with broken faucets (9)

31. Tedious wayfarer (10)

34. Bolt south and run off (6)

35. Musical Greek god's first-class survey round (6)

36. Impressive keyboard (5)

37. The Spanish got into Sri Lanka's biological unit (4)

Down

1. Fight anarchic redcaps? Ed, get out! (5)

2. Hideous moan going around? Run out and desert! (6)

3. Meagre incline (4)

4. Cudgel Society (4)

6. Allot nicer new insect repellent (10)

7. Dilapidated uniform kept in messy diner (6)

9. Tear-drops panic hunting animals (9)

12. Afflict regularly, rapidly (3)

14. Elaborate sweet pie often conic (10)

15. Spontaneous sprite to frolic on Tuesday (9)

16. One upset joker is forbidding (5)

18. Voices agreement aboard steamship (4)

19. Avenue without borders of willow, perhaps (4)

26. Cosset Bond's boss during exam (6)

28. Take advantage of half of justification (3)

29. Dessert of no consequence (6)

30. Deplorable notion to miss tea, I've heard? It causes tears in the kitchen! (5)

32. Deer overshadows last character's rest (4)

33. Navy elite's mammal (4)

Puzzle 54

Across

9. One from France protects Sri Lanka's relative (5)

10. Twin's foolish idle antic (9)

11. Insupportable lawyer tucked into uneaten stew (9)

12. Cleverness to use whiskey, instead of one's muscles (5)

13. Implore English son cleaving big tree (7)

15. Very fashionable seen around Ed from Uppsala, for instance? (7)

16. Shortened words, at length? (13)

20. Old ties found in broken car tubs (7)

22. Doctor operation to allow a tiny tear (7)

23. Porcelain country (5)

24. Elaborate altar base of white stone (9)

26. Open forcibly and take Robin Wild (5,4)

27. Get away from late stages of overture (5)

Down

1. Residential areas' substitutes receiving a back rub (7)

2. Improvised singing? Beat it! (4)

3. Romeo and one German bring back water grass for caribou (8)

4. Naughty! Bad vibes! Shame! (10)

5. Iron tellurium for charity event (4)

6. Secure farm building (6)

7. Wriggly cocoa snail is sporadic (10)

8. Husband set in splint, abandoned statue bases (7)

14. Submerged warships snub armies all over the place (10)

15. Lose self-control, and haul on flower (10)

17. Singled out irregular diastole (8)

18. Drink addition that is around this French baby bear (3,4)

19. Celebrity, Little Edward, got underway (7)

21. State's adult apprentice? Ask ace (6)

24. Composer of *Rule, Britannia* oddly arranged (4)

25. Tense teetotaller went around Australia (4)

Puzzle 55

Across

1. Sips are plentiful on board ship (7)
5. Bolster Mark around us (7)
9. Involving both sides in able trial, confusingly (9)
10. Revamp bridles, without fringes (5)
11. Sky broadcast (3)
12. Letter with fine, single Japanese mushroom (5)
13. An Aussie afternoon with *Arkansas Five-O* (4)
14. Monumental power in crushed ice (4)
17. Decrease the hush on the ice skating arena! (6)
19. Loathing the rostrum, missed entrance (5)
21. The Spanish and African antelope (5)
23. Disqualify the German embracing a scholar (5)
25. Publisher's employee Edward and I go to a rocky hill (6)
27. Hit around hard Thai currency (4)
30. Devours oils, getting energy for foxtrot (4)
32. Surmises a ship, with hesitation, goes to El Salvador (7)
34. Brief expert employed by reprobates (3)
35. Bacterial dish of cooked tripe (5)
36. Estimated massage calms mind (9)
37. Ruination Men return to El Salvador, and Iceland (7)
38. Maria transfixed by doctor's xylophone (7)

Down

1. Douse substitute at French sea quarter (8)
2. Nobler emu strangely represents Victorian capital (9)
3. Ian's after the Italian television from Riga (7)
4. Elegant tree (6)
5. Unusual aims, locking up Alan's sausages (6)
6. Fly up to Somalia first-class, right? (4)
7. Sillier abandoned leader is following (5)
8. Slender pole shaft (6)
13. Friend from Paris is a regular barmaid (3)
15. Fruit's a penny apiece (5)
16. Cryptogram about poem (4)
18. Engineer broke, forgetting Ocean Road's edge (4)

20. Last offer revealed by powerful Tim at Umbria (9)

22. Dubliner's main flower at hotel next to South East Anglia (5,3)

24. Coach covered by rosebushes (3)

26. Own ape arranged a bow, perhaps? (6)

28. First character roams randomly to find perfumes (6)

29. Tenor and little Emily have a two-wheeler for two (6)

31. Carry French man's tribal symbol (5)

33. Yes, Spanish rodent jumps up to lute (5)

34. Old Indian coins for baked treats (4)

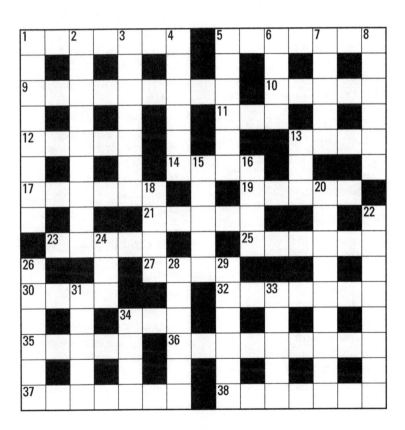

Puzzle 56

Across

1. Settled down around Buck — demolished the old trombone (7)

5. Enhanced humans come from the Cyprus Borg Society (7)

9. Bird alien accepts retrograde energy unit (5)

10. Ten operas developed with a constructed language (9)

11. Insists, donning very French crosses (9)

12. Indian PM's strangely humaner without Ma (5)

14. Canoes floundering, leaving South Pacific, perhaps (5)

15. Concerning the German, after main residue (9)

18. Wrapped up bridge player, residing in occluded building (9)

20. Bud's second-class weaving rig (5)

21. Frenetic hysteria, with Mike in lieu of Penny (5)

22. Eradicated oil, and bashed fudge (9)

24. Prehistoric reptiles rampaging around sis! (9)

26. Propose the chart (5)

27. Fauvist leader's the French man with a siesta composition (7)

28. Son Oscar in pursuit of a lawful request (7)

Down

1. South-western English and French pudding (5)

2. Dreadful carnage near seaweed thickener (11)

3. Resentful northern marshbird (7)

4. Prized step around, confident (9)

5. Manages priests' cloaks (5)

6. Atrociously drub University in African country (7)

7. I got out of the downpour and fled (3)

8. Silence over old Yugoslavia's sauce (5)

13. Mutated hybrid pooch repels water (11)

14. Monster initially only reaches Caranthir (3)

16. Asylums' treatments do shame us (9)

17. Bizarre spirit (3)

19. Copper and saint get stuck into the Spanish grasshoppers (7)

20. Bri's group returns to British port (7)

21. Polite address is reversible (5)

22. Swear at area public transport, Elizabeth! (5)

23. Lived in Lithuania, after wed anew (5)

25. Final tulle (3)

The Answers

This part is where I reveal all! Here, I provide answers to all the puzzles in Part 2.

You'll find that once you have a few words in the grid, you're likely to find cracking the other clues easier. However, if you want to check your answers or are really stuck, then this part is for you!

Chapter **6**
The Answers Revealed!

Here they are. The answers to all your problems!

If you're really stuck on a grid, you can get a hint using these answer grids. Just sneak a peek at part of the answer grid for the puzzle you're working on. Use your hand or a piece of paper to cover most of the grid, if you like, or ask a friend to read out the answer to just one word. Getting one or two of the longer words into the grid can really help you get a foothold on the whole puzzle.

Chapter 3: Easy Peasy Cryptics

Puzzle 1

S	E	E	I	N	G		F	O	R	M	A	L
P		X		O		R		E			O
A	L	T	I	T	U	D	E		L	A	M	B
N		O		L		T			N		B
I	D	L	E		A	B	S	E	N	T	L	Y
S			G		S				E
H	Y	P	O	C	H	O	N	D	R	I	A	C
	A				E		U			O
A	P	P	E	T	I	T	E		G	L	U	M
R		A		M		D		O		I
I	R	I	S		A	T	L	A	N	T	I	C
E		N		G		E		T		A
S	U	T	U	R	E		S	T	R	O	L	L

Puzzle 2

Puzzle 3

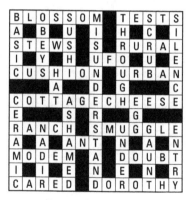

Puzzle 4

Puzzle 5

```
L O C A L   C A P S I Z E
E   O   O   R   R   N   X
P A R A C H U T E   K I P
E   I   U   I   S       O
R E A L M   S E F T H E S
    N     E   N   I   E
S E D A T E   S T A L L S
O   E   R   S     A
P E R F E C T   S E R I F
R     A   Y   T   I   I
A N Y   C E L L U L O S E
N   E   L   U   M   U   N
O Y S T E R S   P O S E D
```

Puzzle 6

```
C A T H A R S I S   C O D
A   A   P   U   T   O   E
T U L I P   L E A F L E T
    L   E   T   I   I   O
H Y E N A   A F R I C A N
I   S   S A N E       A
N U T M E G   T A B L E T
D       A R A L   E   E
S P E C T R E   C L O U D
I   E   I   U   O   N
G A R A G E S   H A I R Y
H   I   E   E   O   N   E
T O E   R E S I L I E N T
```

Puzzle 7

```
T H R O W N   C A S S I S
A   U   E   F   P   T   T
N U B I A   A I R F A R E
N   B   T A S   I   F   A
I R I S H   H E L P F U L
N   S   E   I   E     S
  T H E R M O M E T E R
A   E   N   L   N   S
R E P L I C A   E A G L E
T   R   N   B A G   R   W
H A I R G E L   A W A K E
U   O   O   E   N   V   R
R A R I T Y   A T H E N S
```

Puzzle 8

```
D R E S S U P   M A P L E
R   N   A   A   A   R   A
A N N U L   R E G R E T S
C   U   E   T   I   C   E
U N I T   K I T C H E N S
L     H   C   I   D
A P P R O X I M A T E L Y
  L   L   P   N       O
A M E R I C A N   T O F U
M   A   D   T   I   K   N
B A S M A T I   S L A N G
E   E   Y   O   I   P   E
R U S T S   N A S T I E R
```

Puzzle 9

Puzzle 10

Puzzle 11

Puzzle 12

Puzzle 13

```
G A L A P A G O S . B O A
N . A . L . A . T . O . N
U L T R A . N E U T R O N
. V . C . D . N . E . . O
K N I F F . E A G E R L Y
I . A . B A R S . . . . A
L O N D O N . P H O T O N
O . . . E A S Y . R . . C
B A R N O W L . G L O V E
Y . A . B . L . I . . . U
T O R P E D O . E L B O W
E . E . S . W . N . . . I
S I R . E A S T E R E G G
```

Puzzle 14

```
A L C O T T . A D E L I E
D . O . R . C . O . . . R
V I L L A . R E C L A I M
I . O . W O E . K . . . I
C A M E L . A B S T A I N
E . B . E . M . W . . . E
. C O R R E C T I O N S .
A . E . H . C . I . . . T
B U R M E S E . E A R T H
S . A . L . E B B . . . R
U R C H I N S . E V A D E
R . E . T . E . N . . . A
D O R S E T . A G H A S T
```

Puzzle 15

```
H Y P N O T I S T . A . C
. E . I . U . A . A R C H
T A L C . N E X T . I . E
. R . E . G . E X A M S .
C . B R A S S . N . . . T
H U E . . T O B O G G A N
O . E . R E F E R . A . U
C A R D I N A L . M A T .
O . V . S I N C E . . . S
L U N G E . T . O . . . M
A . R E N T . R E E K . .
T W I N . F . L . F . N .
E . L . S T R E N U O U S
```

Puzzle 16

```
M O T E L S . A F R A I D
O . E . W . C . I . . . E
D I M I N I S H . T O W N
E . P . N . E . L . . . S
L O O M . D E S C R I B E
. . O . L . . . A . . . .
. A B O V E G R O U N D .
. W . . A . M . . . . . .
T E A S P O O N . P L O T
W . R . F . S . A . . . H
I T E M . F L A M I N G O
N . N . E . C . C . . . R
E R A S E R . K O R E A N
```

Puzzle 17

Puzzle 19

Puzzle 18

Puzzle 20

Puzzle 21

```
A M P L I F I E S   B O W
I   U   M   N   W   I   H
M I N I M   C H I A N T I
  G   O   O   N   G   M
S T E E R   M A G N E T S
E   N   A P E S       I
M E T T L E   I T A L I C
A       S C A R   U   A
P A R A S O L   A N G E L
H   A   H   I   C   G
O M I C R O N   T R A S H
R   S   U   G   O   G   I
E V E   B O Y F R I E N D
```

Puzzle 22

```
B R A G S   F I T N E S S
E   M   W   R   A   R   A
R E P R I M A N D   R I P
E   E   N   P   P     I
T E R S E   P R O M I S E
    S     E   L   M   N
G R A S P S   T E A P O T
O   N   A   E     R
B U D D I E S   C R E A M
L     N   C   H   C   O
E R G   T R A D I T I O N
T   O   E   P   L   S   E
S C O U R G E   E N E M Y
```

Puzzle 23

```
D I S T U R B   C I T E S
R   E   G   R   A   E   L
A P P A L   I M M E R S E
W   A   Y   T   I   R   E
I L L S   L I P S T I C K
N     A   S   O   E
G R A N D C H I L D R E N
  N   H   M   E     E
G R A C E F U L   C L O G
A   E   S   S   E   U   L
V A M P I R E   T E N S E
E   I   V   U   O   A   C
L U C R E   M I N A R E T
```

Puzzle 24

```
  S   K   I O N   T   G
P O D I U M   E V A D E S
  N   O   P   W   I   L
M A N S I O N   C L E A R
  T   K   S     O   T
D A D     I N F E R I O R
O     A   N   U   S   A
C A R D I G A N   H O T
  C   D     N   F   F
S T A R T   G I R A F F E
  I   E   E   E   B   E
C O R S E T   S A L I N E
  N   S   C O T   E   D
```

Puzzle 25

Chapter 4: Challenging Cryptics

Puzzle 26

Puzzle 27

Puzzle 28

Puzzle 29

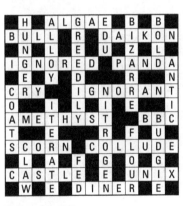

Puzzle 30

Puzzle 31

Puzzle 32

Puzzle 33

Puzzle 34

Puzzle 35

Puzzle 36

```
U S H E R S . R A I S I N
N . I . A E . . . T . . E
C O N S U M E S . I O W A
A . D . U . I . . I . . R
P L U G . R A N S A C K S
. . A . A . . . . . . I .
. D E S T I N A T I O N .
. A . . . . N . M . . . .
I M M E R S E D . P A I R
C . E . . U . R . C . . A
I S L E . P R O P E R T Y
N . O . . E . I . E . . O
G I N G E R . D A M S O N
```

Puzzle 37

```
C R E A M S . A D R I F T
L . L . A . I . A . C . A
I S A A C . M A C B E T H
N . T . A L P . H . N . I
C L I M B . R E A L I S T
H . O . R . O . . O . . I
. I N T E R V I E W E D .
S . O . . E . P . M . . S
T A N T R U M . A M B L E
A . I . O . E M U . R . A
R E G I M E N . L E A S T
C . H . E . T . E . C . E
H O T D O G . A T T E N D
```

Puzzle 38

```
. B . E M B E R . S . B
K E E L . O . A N T L E R
. R . G . T . G . A . R
C A R A W A Y . F U D G E
. T . R . N . . N . . N
F E W . I N D E C E N T
A . O . S . I . H . . E
D I A B E T E S . J A R
E . S . . A . L . L
D A T E S . A S C E T I C
. S . R . E . T . V . E
S H O V E L . E . E R N E
. Y . E . M U R A L . S
```

Puzzle 39

```
D E M O N . R A I N I E R
O . E . I . E . N . R . E
R I D I C U L E S . E O S
I . I . H . A . E . . . O
C Y C L E . T A C T F U L
. I . . E . T . A . . A V
C A N A D A . P S Y C H E
A . E . I . B . . T . . .
M U S I C A L . A D O R N
P . . T . A . E . R . A
E R A . A D M I S S I O N
R . D . T . E . O . E . N
S U S P E N D . P A S T Y
```

Puzzle 36 **Puzzle 37**

Puzzle 38 **Puzzle 39**

Puzzle 40

Puzzle 41

Puzzle 42

Puzzle 43

Chapter 5: Treacherous Cryptics

Puzzle 44

Puzzle 46

Puzzle 45

Puzzle 47

Puzzle 48

Puzzle 49

Puzzle 50

Puzzle 51

Puzzle 52

```
M A L I C E   E S C A P A D E
Y O   A P   O   S   P     M
C O I N T R E A U   P U P A E
O   R   A   R   T     E   N
L I E   S O F T H E A R T E D
O     T   E   A   D   I   8
G A S T R I C   U N M A S K
Y   T   O   T   S   O   E G
  T A I P E I   T E N D R I L
A   G   H   O   R   I     I
C E N T E N N I A L S   T U M
C   A   I   L   H   R     P
O C T E T   S C I M I T A R S
R   E   A   T   A   N   D   E
D I S B U R S E   A G R E E D
```

Puzzle 53

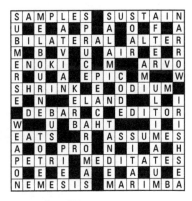

```
S   M     L A C E   A C O R N
C L A U S E   L   P   I   U
R   R   A   U   R E T A I N
A B O M I N A B L E   R   N
P   O     I   D   O   E
  E N C H I L A D A   N O D S
T   O   M   L   T H E     A
R A I N   P H O T O   L A D Y
E     F I R   O   R   L   S
E P E E   O B F U S C A T E
  A   C   M   S     R   O
  M   T   P E D E S T R I A N
S P R I N T   O   E   F   I
E   O   U   Z   A P O L L O
G R A N D   C E L L     E   N
```

Puzzle 54

```
S   S   R   M   F   S   O   P
U N C L E   I D E N T I C A L
B   A   I   S   T   A   C   I
U N T E N A B L E   B R A W N
R     D   E     L   S     T
B E S E E C H   S W E D I S H
S   U   E   A   N     O   S
  A B B R E V I A T I O N S
I   M     E   P   S   A   S
C R A V A T S   D R O P L E T
E   R   L     R   L     A
C H I N A   A L A B A S T E R
U   N   S   R   G   T   A   T
B R E A K I N T O   E L U D E
E   S   A   E   N   D   T   D
```

Puzzle 55

```
S A M P L E S   S U S T A I N
U   E   A   P   A   O   F   A
B I L A T E R A L   A L T E R
M   B   V   U   A I R   E   R
E N O K I   C   M   A R V O
R   U   A   E P I C   M   W
S H R I N K   E   O D I U M
E   N     E L A N D   L   I
  D E B A R   C   E D I T O R
W   U   B A H T   I   I
E A T S   R   A S S U M E S
A   O   P R O   N   I   A   H
P E T R I   M E D I T A T E S
O   E   E   A   E   A   U   E
N E M E S I S   M A R I M B A
```

Puzzle 56

About the Author

Denise Sutherland is an Australian author, graphic designer, editor, indexer and puzzle writer. She is a member of the Institute of Professional Editors and the ACT Writers Centre.

Denise has been fascinated with puzzles and mysteries of all kinds since she was a child — not surprisingly, murder mysteries are her favourite novels to read. In recent years, she has been a regular on ABC radio, putting cryptic clues to the audience.

This book is Denise's fourth title in the For Dummies series; her previous books are *Solving Cryptic Crosswords For Dummies*, *Word Searches For Dummies* and *Cracking Codes and Cryptograms For Dummies* (written with Mark Koltko-Rivera). She also writes non-fiction, especially in the scientific and medical fields. Denise's website and blog can be found at sutherland-studios.com.au, and she would love to chat with you on Facebook at www.facebook.com/AussieNisi.

She lives in Canberra with her husband, and has two grown-up children and two cute chihuahuas. She loves knitting, cooking, and solving cryptic crosswords.

Author's Acknowledgements

Endless thanks to my husband Ralph and kids for their support, and for putting up with my insane working hours and scrambled brain while writing this book. A special thank you to my darling daughter Jenny, for creating so many yummy meals. Her cooking skills have definitely levelled up!

My gratitude also to Deborah Green for her cheery and sterling work as technical editor on this book. Thanks also to Ross Beresford, for his invaluable Wordplay Wizard software.

Publisher's Acknowledgements

We're proud of this book; please send us your comments through our online registration form located at www.dummies.com/register.

Some of the people who helped bring this book to market include the following:

Acquisitions, Editorial and Media Development

Project Editor: Danielle Karvess

Acquisitions Editors: Rebecca Crisp, Clare Weber

Technical Editor: Deborah Green

Production

Proofreader: Jenny Scepanovic

Every effort has been made to trace the ownership of copyright material. Information that enables the publisher to rectify any error or omission in subsequent editions is welcome. In such cases, please contact the Permissions Section of John Wiley & Sons Australia, Ltd.